**Sing a New Song
to the Lord**

To Alison a.k.a "lurch",

wishing you hours of fun
developing your hymnology
with uncle Bouncy

lots of love

Daryl

Sing a New Song to the Lord

The Power and Potential of Hymns

BRIAN CASTLE

DARTON · LONGMAN + TODD

FOR JANE, JAMIE, SARAH AND BETHAN
WITH LOVE AND THANKS

First published in 1994 by
Darton, Longman and Todd Ltd
1 Spencer Court
140–142 Wandsworth High Street
London SW18 4JJ

ISBN 0–232–52005–4

A catalogue record for this book is available
from the British Library

Photypeset by Intype, London
Printed and bound in Great Britain
by Page Bros, Norwich

Contents

Acknowledgements

I would like to thank the following: Michael Ball of Sutton Baptist Church, John Bell of the Iona Community, Brother Dirk of the Taizé Community, Colin Thompson of St Catherine's College, Oxford, Alan Luff of Birmingham Cathedral, Ian Bradley of Aberdeen University, John Garton and my staff colleagues at Ripon College, Cuddesdon for their advice, knowledge and wisdom as I was writing this book; Geoffrey Wrayford of Minehead, archivist for the Hymn Society Bulletins, for generously giving me access to this valuable resource; Violet Nyirenda and Edgars Kasongo from Chingola, Zambia, for translating the Zambian hymns and revealing their great riches to me; John White of St George's, Windsor, who spent a great deal of time and energy reading and commenting on the chapters sent to him.

Thanks are due to those groups and congregations who have been willing to use hymns within discussion groups and have given so much, thereby helping me formulate and test some of the ideas found here. Special thanks go to the parishes of North Petherton and Moorland, Somerset, and the students of Ripon College, Cuddesdon who have had more than their fair share of exposure. Needless to say, I bear full responsibility for the shortcomings within this book.

Finally, I would like to thank my wife Jane for acting as an unpaid research assistant, sounding board and encourager – it is to her and our children Jamie, Sarah and Bethan that this book is dedicated.

* * *

Thanks are due to the following for permission to quote copyright material: Mr J. M. Barnes for 'I Love My Lord'; Christopher Bradnock for 'Cradle, O Lord, in your arms everlasting'; Canterbury Press for 'Lord of beauty, thine the splendour'; Copycare, PO Box 77, Hailsham, BN27 3EF, for 'I love you, Lord' by Laurie Klein, copyright © 1978 Maranatha! Music; Darton, Longman and Todd for *The Jerusalem Bible*, published and copyright 1966, 1967 and 1968 by Darton, Longman and Todd Ltd and Doubleday & Co Inc.; Timothy Dudley-Smith for 'Tell out my soul'; Hope Publishing Company for 'God of Freedom, God of Justice' by Shirley Erena Murray, copyright © 1992 by

Introduction

Hymns are the folk-song of the church militant

Erik Routley

It all began in Brixton. When working and worshipping in this multi-cultural part of South London the question arose as to how we could communicate with one another about God. We all came from different backgrounds, many from different countries and cultures and we understood words in different ways. We even understood worship in different ways: the vitality of Black Pentecostal worship was a contrast to the formality of Anglican worship. The atmosphere created by singing accompanied by drums was different from that accompanied by the organ – not better, but different. Were we worshipping the same God?

This question lived on through theological training and ordination to the priesthood and surfaced again in the Copperbelt of Northern Zambia. I was serving a parish with one church in the centre of the town plus a number of satellite congregations scattered in communities, known as townships, which had sprung up around the edge of town. The town centre congregation was truly multi-cultural with 85 per cent being Zambian (drawn from different Zambian tribes with different languages), 10 per cent Asian (from India, Sri Lanka and the Philippines) and 5 per cent European. The only common language was English, but this was the language of the minority, which meant that the majority of the congregation communicated with God, in worship, in a language which was not their mother tongue.

The township churches presented a different picture. The congregations were all Zambian and the language (or, on occasion, languages) was spoken and sung fluently by all. The result was worship that was vibrant and which communicated a sense of the presence of God to those who were not familiar with the language. The youth choirs sang and moved to the hymns which they (or a neighbouring choir) had composed themselves, and the congregation sang their more traditional hymns. In the town centre church we began experimenting. Although the majority of the service continued to be conducted in English, we would occasionally have prayers in Malayalam or Tamil (languages of South India and Sri Lanka). We regularly sang the 'Lamb of God' in ci-Bemba, a Zambian language and we would sing hymns in another Zambian language.

Although we continued with hymns from *Hymns Ancient and Modern*, we would be open to hymns from other English speaking traditions. Members of the congregation felt a great comfort that they had been able, within an act of corporate worship, to communicate with God in their own language, images and thought forms. Even if it was only for one minute they felt that they had really worshipped. A willingness to be part of and experience such worship benefited us all as people felt affirmed that their culture and understanding of God were being acknowledged, while the rest of us learnt a great deal simply by listening.

If there is a question of communicating about God *between* cultures, so too there is a question *within* cultures. Some people have middle-class backgrounds, others are more working-class. Some people place more stress on the emotional side of personality, others place more on the rational. Some people feel that they benefit from society, others feel that they are victims of society. Such experiences affect the way that we approach and view God and have implications for communication and worship.

This book is about giving an opportunity for those in the pew to have a say within the worship they attend and a voice in theological debate outside of it. A creative use of hymns is one way of providing this voice. The book is written from an Anglican perspective, though with an openness to the riches of other traditions and cultures. At the beginning we explore the power of hymns, seeing their relationship with culture, their role within theology and their potential for communicating 'popular' theology. With these themes to the fore, we have a brief glance at the historical development of hymns, and consider in more depth the last thirty 'explosive' years, which have seen a phenomenal hymn output at an unsettling time for Church and world. We discuss hymns within worship and liturgy and also suggest ways in which they can be used without worship as a means of communicating and exploring the faith. In the last two chapters we consider the direction in which hymns are moving, reflecting on the thorny issue of how we assess hymns and asking what are the implications for the Church, theology and mission if the methods suggested here are taken seriously. Although I raise the question of what makes a good hymn, it is certainly not my main task to provide a critique on the quality of hymns, but rather to comment on them for what they are, wondering why their potential has never been realized.

At the heart of this book is a conviction that everybody has some insight about God but may not feel they have the means to express it. Song is a universal medium of communication: hymns, used creatively and reflectively, offer a universal means of communicating the faith. We may not always understand, but we can listen.

1

The Power of the Hymn

The hymn provides the most resonant evocation of religious feeling in Britain: far more so than liturgy. The Bible itself hardly rivals it, even among the most biblicist of believers. The hymn is the most central item in the religion of Britain and the singing of 'Abide with me' at the Cup Final or 'Jerusalem' at the last night of the Promenade Concerts remains a witness to its unique place in popular affection.

David Martin

For the vast majority of the population hymns are their only contact with formal religion. Hymns are remembered from school assemblies, weddings, baptisms and funerals. They are remembered from great state occasions when it is the words of hymns that have the power to set the emotional as well as the spiritual tone of the event. Hymns are sung at football matches, at the last night of the Proms and in the showers after rugby matches. A 1989 poll showed that 62 per cent of Britain's entire population watches Christian television programmes regularly.[1] Nearly half of that 62 per cent watch ever popular programmes featuring hymns: an article in *The Times* in 1989 pointed out that while every Sunday morning nearly eight million people throughout Britain gather in churches where they sing hymns of praise, another eight million (and research shows that they are not just the same people) watch *Songs of Praise* or *Highway* on television and hundreds of thousands more tune in to radio broadcasts of hymns like *Sunday Half-Hour*.[2] ITVs *Highway* was axed from the television schedule in 1993, provoking 1,400 aggrieved viewers to send letters of complaint ('the most for a single issue') to the Independent Television Commission.[3] All this points to the accuracy of Ian Bradley's words in *The Penguin Book of Hymns*:

> They [hymns] are perhaps the strongest expression of the folk religion which is still deeply embedded in our so-called secular society. For many people they provide a more familiar and accessible source of teaching about the Christian faith than the Bible. There can be few who do not know the opening verses of 'There is a green hill far away' or 'Abide with me.' Half-remembered verses from childhood hymns and choruses remain a great source of inspiration and comfort to many who would not count themselves as regular churchgoers or committed believers.[4]

Yet despite all of this and the fact that hymn-singing is common to the majority of Christians, the potential of hymns has not been exploited. Hymns have not been taken seriously as a means by which those who have not received formal training in theology, yet have much to communicate about the Christian faith, can enter and take part in theological debate alongside theological professionals.

All of this will be discussed. But first, what is a hymn?

St Augustine describes a hymn in this way:

> Do you know what a hymn is? It is singing with the praise of God. If you praise God and do not sing, you utter no hymn. If you sing and praise not God, you utter no hymn. If you praise anything which does not pertain to the praise of God, though in singing you praise, you utter no hymn.[5]

'Singing with the praise of God' describes simply and succinctly what is in the heart of our finest hymn-writers and there are many jewels of hymnody which reach this height. This definition also enables us to include other songs of praise in addition to the traditional metrical hymn: for instance, psalms, Taizé music and choruses which have become more widely sung over the last thirty years. Any song which makes the singer aware of God's presence and lifts the singer in praise of the Deity is a hymn. Praising God is a broad definition of a hymn, but they serve many purposes and fulfil many functions.

Hymns, like their antecedents, the psalms, are a way that

human beings try to respond to and make sense of faith in God. The ever-popular 'Abide With Me' reveals one man coming to terms with death in the light of his beliefs: its popularity is an indication that he is articulating the struggle for many people. The hymn was the work of Anglican priest Henry Francis Lyte and was probably written in 1820 after he visited an old friend, Augustus le Hunte, who was terminally ill. The dying Hunte repeated on a number of occasions the phrase 'Abide with me' and these words made such an impression on Lyte that he felt the need to construct the hymn around them. For the opening of the hymn, he used the incident recorded in Luke 24.29, where the disciples meet Christ (though not recognizing him) on the road to Emmaus and ask him to stay with them ('Abide with us'). When Lyte was coming to the end of his own life in 1847, his mind returned to this hymn which he gave to a relative who had it published. Clearly the hymn which, for Lyte, made some sense of faith in the face of Hunte's death also helped Lyte come to some understanding of his own. 'Abide With Me' is frequently placed in the 'evening' section of hymn books, but Victorian hymn-writer John Ellerton, sensing how the hymn reflects its origins, complains that this is a:

> misapprehension of the true meaning of a hymn by those among whom it is popular; for a very little consideration will suffice to shew that there is not throughout the hymn the slightest allusion to the close of the natural day . . . It is far better to be sung at funerals, as it was beside the grave of Professor Maurice; but it is almost too intense and personal for ordinary congregational use.[6]

Hymns have also been written for more didactic purposes. Mrs Cecil Frances Alexander, wife of the Bishop of Derry who later became the Primate of all Ireland, wrote hymns for children in the Sunday Schools in which she taught. She was wanting to explain to the children the basic doctrines of Christianity, in particular the meaning of the Apostles' Creed. So, she wrote 'All Things Bright and Beautiful' to explain the opening words 'I believe in God the Father Almighty, Maker of heaven and earth'; 'Once in Royal David's City' to explain 'Born of the Virgin Mary'; and 'There is a Green Hill Far

Away' to illuminate the phrase 'was crucified under Pontius Pilate'. The hymn 'O Jesus, I Have Promised' was written by Revd John Ernest Bode in 1866 for the confirmation of his three children. The opening lines make reference to the promises made at confirmation.

Hymns also breathe life into scriptural passages. Charles Wesley published in 1762 *Short Hymns on Selected Passages of Scripture*. Probably the most popular hymn from this (and a number are still sung) is 'O Thou who Camest from Above' which is based on Leviticus 6.13:

> An undying fire is always to burn on the altar; it must not go out.

Wesley is comparing the faith of the Christian believer to the Jewish practice of burnt offerings where the fire is kept alive until the offering is completely consumed.

As well as breathing life into scriptural passages, references to the way that God has worked in the past imply an appeal that God may work in a similar way in the present. So, the spiritual 'Go Down, Moses' is asking that the same spirit of God which released the Israelites from slavery may also release the enslaved black population of America:

> When Israel was in Egypt's land,
> Let my people go.
> Oppressed so hard they could not stand,
> Let my people go.
> Go down, Moses,
> Go down, to Egypt's land.
> Tell ole Pharaoh.
> Let my people go.

Hymns free the emotions to engage with faith, enabling it to be apprehended at deep levels of the human psyche. On a number of occasions I have been with people who through mental illness or senility have been unable to communicate in the conventional way; however, they have been able to sing hymns learnt many years before. Certain situations may 'trigger' hymns in the memory: death and bereavement often bring hymns into mind, just as times of happiness and elation. I was told by a former soldier how the hymn 'Rock of Ages, Cleft for

Me' provided reassurance during a border operation in Northern Ireland. With his fellow soldiers he had to dig and camouflage himself in a hillside where he remained for days. They were under constant threat of attack, but he derived comfort at the most difficult times from the words:

> Rock of ages, cleft for me,
> Let me hide myself in thee.

Hymns have provided a channel of emotions for churches of the reformed tradition. Hymns have played such a significant role in reformed churches because they have replaced the 'art' in Catholic churches. In his very good, though idiosyncratic book, *The Hymns of Wesley and Watts* (published in 1942), Congregationalist Bernard L. Manning, making no secret of his prejudices, comments:

> if we use no crucifix, no stations of the cross, no processions, no banners, no incense, you must attribute it not to the fancy that we have neither need nor understanding of what these things represent. We do not use these things because our hymns revive the sacred scene and stir the holy emotions with a power and a purity denied to all but the greatest craftsman. There are pictures of the crucifixion that rival, and perhaps excel, the passion hymns of Watts and Wesley; but those pictures are to be sought in distant lands by the few and the wealthy for a few moments only. The hymn-book offers masterpieces for all who have an ear to hear, every day and in every place, to every worshipper. When I am informed that Dissenting worship is bare and cold, making no appeal to the emotions because it does not employ the tawdry and flashy productions of fifth-rate ecclesiastical art-mongers, I am at a loss for an answer. I am only at a loss, when I am asked to explain why, holding these treasures, we turn so often from them – the great passionate, emotional hymns – to the pedestrian rhymers of ethical commonplaces.[7]

As well as enabling emotional expression, hymns allow articulation of the sexual content of the human–divine relationship. For example, the metaphors of love, longing, panting and ecstasy are not uncommon in hymns:

> O Love, how deep! how broad! how high!
> It fills the heart with ecstasy.

In 'O God of Hosts, the Mighty Lord' we read:

> My longing soul faints with desire
> to view thy blest abode;
> my panting heart and flesh cry out
> for Thee the living God.

In 'Lo! He Comes with Clouds Descending' there is a stress, for some too great a stress, on the wounds of Christ:

> Those dear tokens of His Passion
> Still His dazzling Body bears,
> Cause of endless exultation
> To His ransom'd worshippers;
> With what rapture
> Gaze we on those glorious scars!

Hymns can be vehicles of doctrine and aids to devotion. Methodists have traditionally used hymns in the former way and Anglicans in the latter way. Hymns frequently make doctrine palatable and accessible to those who feel alienated by the propositional language of the creeds. For example, many would say, though not easily relate to, the words of the Nicene Creed:

> God of God, Light of Light, Very God of Very God, begotten, not made, being of one substance with the Father, by whom all things were made: who for us men, and for our salvation came down from heaven, and was incarnate by the Holy Ghost of the Virgin Mary, and was made man.

Far more could sing the equivalent in 'Hark! The Herald-angels Sing':

> Veiled in flesh the Godhead see:
> hail, the incarnate Deity,
> pleased as Man with man to dwell,
> Jesus, our Emmanuel.

'We Hail thy Presence Glorious' feeds the worshipper's devotional life as it reflects on the sacrament of Holy Communion:

We hail thy presence glorious,
O Christ our great High Priest . . .

O living bread from heaven,
Jesu, our Saviour good,
who thine own self hast given
to be our souls' true food . . .

Just as hymns can express doctrine in a didactic way, so too they may express it in a more polemical vein. In 1861 William Colenso, a Cornishman who had been appointed Bishop of Natal, wrote a commentary of the epistle to the Romans in which he raised eyebrows within the Church by asking critical questions about the Church's sacramental habits. However, in 1862 he was regarded by many as heretical when he published his book *Critical Examination of the Pentateuch*. In this work, Colenso was studying the Old Testament in the light of his missionary experience and came to what was (at that time) a staggering theory that Moses did not write the Pentateuch (the first five books of the Bible) but that they were post-prophetic forgeries. The Archbishop of Capetown deposed Colenso from his bishopric because of the scandal that erupted from his views, but Colenso, after taking legal advice, disregarded the Archbishop's action and continued to minister in his diocese. In England opinion was against Colenso whose resignation was demanded by the majority of English bishops in support of the Archbishop of Capetown. Colenso's opinions are not regarded as at all radical now, nor were they radical then to some German theologians, but they were sufficient to cause a schism. Not only did Colenso continue his ministry in Natal until his death in 1883, but even after that there was a group which refused to support the legally consecrated bishop. The schism was not properly resolved until A. Hamilton Baynes was appointed Bishop of Natal in 1891.

Meanwhile, Samuel John Stone, curate at Haggerston, London, felt very strongly the grief of schism perpetrated by Colenso. Upset that the Bible was being robbed of its authority, he wrote the hymn 'The Church's One Foundation'. The first verse has clear references to the passage which inspired the hymn, Ephesians 5.24–6:

> and as the Church submits to Christ, so should wives to their husbands, in everything. Husbands should love their wives just as Christ loved the Church and sacrificed himself for her to make her holy. He made her clean by washing her in water with a form of words,

and the second verse makes direct reference to the Colenso controversy:

> The Church's one foundation
> is Jesus Christ, her Lord;
> She is his new creation
> by water and the word;
> From heaven he came and sought her
> to be his holy Bride,
> With his own blood he bought her
> and for her life he died.
>
> Though with a scornful wonder
> men see her sore opprest,
> By schisms rent asunder,
> by heresies distrest,
> Yet saints their watch are keeping,
> their cry goes up – 'How long?'
> And soon the night of weeping
> shall be the morn of song.

There is a long and noble tradition of hymns providing a critique for the community. Hymns lead the way in rectifying unsatisfactory conditions and crystallizing new demands. The psalms are forthright in their criticisms, as in Psalm 15 which finds some behaviour so unacceptable as to prevent entry into God's sacred presence. Who can enter God's temple or live on his holy mountain? The psalmist replies:

> The man whose way of life is blameless,
> who always does what is right,

> who speaks the truth from his heart,
> whose tongue is not used for slander,
>
> who does no wrong to his fellow,
> casts no discredit on his neighbour,
> looks with contempt on the reprobate,
> but honours those who fear Yahweh;
>
> who stands by his pledge at any cost,
> does not ask interest on loans,
> and cannot be bribed to victimise the innocent.
> – If a man does all this, nothing can ever shake him.

Such critique is taken up implicitly in some hymns, but explicitly in others, like G. K. Chesterton's 'O God of Earth and Altar':

> O God of earth and altar,
> Bow down and hear our cry,
> Our earthly rulers falter,
> Our people drift and die;
> The walls of gold entomb us,
> The swords of scorn divide,
> Take not thy thunder from us,
> But take away our pride.

We shall be seeing how this is true of hymns in African as well as Western culture, thereby providing an expression of deep-seated feelings not permissibly verbalised in other contexts. As anthropologist Hugh Tracey says in an article on the Chopi tribe:

> You can say publicly in songs what you cannot say privately to a man's face, and so this is one of the ways African society takes to maintain a spiritually healthy community.[8]

Hymns also enable a community to express its contradictions and ambivalences. In Mrs Alexander's hymn for St Andrew the Apostle, 'Jesus Calls Us; O'er the Tumult', there is an explicit condemnation of money and material wealth:

> Jesus calls us from the worship
> Of the vain world's golden store . . .

Yet the same collection of hymns (*Hymns Ancient and Modern*) conceptualizes heaven, the place where men and women will rest with God, in terms of great wealth in the hymn 'For Thee, O Dear, Dear Country':

> With jasper glows thy bulwarks,
> Thy streets with emeralds blaze;
> The sardius and the topaz
> Unite in thee their rays;
> Thine ageless walls are bonded
> With amethyst unpriced . . .

Hymns also allow the worshipper to vent feelings against God and raise questions about God's existence or the extent to which God cares. The psalm which even the New Testament acknowledges utters a cry of despair at being abandoned by God is Psalm 22:

> My God, my God, why have you deserted me?
> How far from saving me, the words that I groan!
> I call all day, my God, but you never answer,
> all night long I call and cannot rest.

Doubt is also well expressed in the Iona hymn 'Finding God' which begins with the line 'Where can we find the God who made and wants us for his very own?':

> God's found where he was set aside –
> The last upset where faith went blind,
> The fond, fake image still embraced
> In the school playground of our mind.

The earliest hymns in the Christian tradition were primarily 'objective', praising God by focusing in awe and wonder solely upon the sacred story with little, if any, mention of human beings. Where humanity is present, it appears collectively. 'Vexilla Regis' was the work of Venantius Fortunatus, Bishop of Poitiers in the sixth century, and was meant to be sung in a procession bearing a fragment of the true cross. The hymn was translated by the nineteenth-century hymn-writer J. M. Neale as 'The Royal Banners Forward Go':

The royal banners forward go,
The Cross shines forth in mystic glow;
Where He is flesh, our flesh Who made,
Our sentence bore, our ransom paid.

There whilst He hung, His sacred Side
By soldier's spear was open'd wide,
To cleanse us in the precious flood
Of Water mingled with His Blood.

Fulfill'd is now what David told
In true prophetic song of old,
How God the heathen's King should be:
For God is reigning from the tree.

By contrast, one of the main features of modern chorus hymns is their subjectivity and outpouring of emotion. The sacred story is not always explicit:

I love you, Lord, and I lift my voice
to worship you. O my soul rejoice,
Take joy, my King, In what you hear,
may it be a sweet, sweet sound in your ear.

The reason for the different approaches was that the hymns were meeting the very different needs of the communities for which they were written. The latter hymn encourages a deeper commitment to God by the individual who was singing it. The former hymn would have been written for a community of monks already committed and so they would be able to ponder over the sacred story to which they had made vows of obedience. Although in one sense the hymn is objective because it reflects upon the sacred story and does not interpret how people should live as a result of the reflections, in another sense it is far from objective because the Latin words in which it was written were charged with contemporary associations reflecting the situation and theological approach of the writer. The subsequent translations of this hymn reflect the translator's concerns. Neale originally translated the third line of the third verse 'Amidst the nations' (which is close to the Latin 'dicendo

nationibus'). However, the compilers of the 1861 *Hymns
Ancient and Modern* changed it to 'How God the heathen's King
should be' reflecting the nineteenth-century missionary thrust
and asserting that God was the king of the whole world. Percy
Dearmer, editor of *Songs of Praise* (first published in 1925),
adapted the first two lines of the second verse to:

> There was he slain in noble youth,
> There suffered to maintain the truth.

These lines reflect the nationalist emphasis in *Songs of Praise*
and hint back to the First World War, urging the singers to
make a link between the sacrifices made there and that made
on the cross at Calvary.

Another 'objective' hymn containing clear contemporary
associations is Martin Luther's 'A Safe Stronghold Our God is
Still'. Luther (1482–1546) who was instrumental in the Reformation wrote this great hymn of defiance against the evil of the
world with his battle against the Roman Catholic Church firmly
in mind. The lines

> The ancient prince of hell
> hath risen with purpose fell . . .

refer to the devil, but singers would have recognized an allusion
to the Pope. It was most probably written in 1529 for the Diet
of Speyer where German princes protested to the Emperor
about the loss of religious freedom; the first four lines of the
second verse would have sounded like a veiled threat:

> With force of arms we nothing can,
> Full soon were we down-ridden;
> But for us fights the proper Man
> Who God himself hath bidden.
> Ask ye who is this same?
> Christ Jesus is His Name . . .

From this it can be seen how hymns contain the hymn-
writer's interpretation of the faith, which, in turn, is conditioned
by the period in which the writer lives and the background
from which the writer comes. This can also be seen in Charles
Wesley's hymn, 'Forth in thy Name, O Lord, I Go' where he

describes work as an 'easy yoke' (v. 4). This was the view of a university-educated clergyman who would have had some control of his time-table: such a view would not have been shared by many farm labourers. This hymn would have been popular among those who are in control over others, the squires and factory-owners, but certainly not among the victims of their control, the farm labourers and factory-workers. In a similar way, there can be little doubt about the way Richard Jones was influenced by the culture and technology of the mid-twentieth century upon which he reflects in this hymn:

> God of concrete, God of steel,
> God of piston and of wheel,
> God of pylon, God of steam,
> God of girder and of beam,
> God of atom, God of mine,
> all the world of power is thine.

Musicologist A. P. Merriam has systematically studied the relationship of songs against their background and acknowledges that they reflect the culture of which they are a part. Merriam writes:

> Through the study of song texts it may well be possible to strike quickly through the protective mechanisms to arrive at an understanding of the ethos of the culture and to gain some perspectives of psychological problems and processes peculiar to it . . . Mythology, legend and history are found in song texts and song is frequently used as an enculturative device . . . Songs provide the student of human behaviour with some of the richest material he has available for analysis, but their full potential remains yet to be exploited.[9]

Hymns are sacred songs and fulfil the same function in regard to the Christian faith as songs do to culture. Some hymns maintain and transmit the culture of the 'few', which may be the dominant culture imposed upon the majority. Other hymns maintain and transmit a more popular culture. There is no suggestion that 'popular' culture is homogeneous since many different strands and belief-patterns constitute any culture, but 'popular' is understood here in general terms as that to which the many can assent. In both senses, hymns are Christian folk-songs. Folksongs keep alive and transmit a culture by highlighting an event or an aspect of life of common concern using contemporary symbols and language.

As Christian folk-songs, many hymns are expressions of popular theology. Doctrine expresses what the Church feels its people *should* believe, hymns express what people *do* believe. For example, the Church traditionally teaches that after death Christians should look forward to a reunion with God and, in the company of the saints, enjoy God's presence for eternity. But many hymns provide a different emphasis as in this hymn, found in *Sacred Songs and Solos*, one of the bestselling hymn books ever published:

> With friends on earth we meet in gladness,
> While swift the moments fly,
> Yet ever comes the thought of sadness,
> That we must say 'Good-bye.'
>
> *Chorus*: We'll never say 'Goodbye' in heav'n,
> We'll never say 'Good-bye;'
> In that fair land of joy and song,
> We'll never say 'Good-bye.'
>
> How joyful is the hope that lingers,
> When loved ones cross death's sea,
> That we, when all earth's toils are ended,
> With them shall ever be.

Even in *Hymns Ancient and Modern*, which is linked more closely to the establishment (Church and state), one finds in the hymn 'God the Father, God the Son':

> Where with loved ones gone before
> We may love Thee and adore.

Folk-songs depend for their existence upon an audience which is willing to listen, be moved, comforted, challenged and can identify with the story. So too hymns need to be able to speak to their singers in a similar way. However, we have seen how Charles Wesley's 'Forth in thy Name, O Lord, I Go' was

more acceptable to one group of society than another. It would
have reinforced and given 'divine' acceptability to the ruling
classes' life-styles and sacred sanction to the status quo,
whereas those in the labouring classes would have found it
difficult to identify not only with such sentiments, but also
with the establishment which allowed them to be expressed in
song. Similarly, Evangelicals may sing hymns with which Anglo-
Catholics do not identify and Traditionalists may sing hymns
with which Charismatics do not identify. A hymn, then, defines
and can tell us something about the community in which it is
popular and acceptable as well as something about the community which refuses to sing it. The renowned hymnologist
Erik Routley develops this point in the Introduction to his book
An English-Speaking Hymnal Guide:

> from one [hymn] book alone you are already learning some-
> thing about church history: from two, you begin to learn
> something about the different church traditions. Who can really
> explain the difference in England between 'high church' and
> 'low church'? Despairing of any reliable definitions, all you
> need do is open the 'English Hymnal' and lay it alongside the
> 'Anglican Hymnal' (1965), and there you have, if not a defi-
> nition, at least a picture of the difference . . . Many have only
> the obscurest notions of what is really different between Ameri-
> can Methodists and American Presbyterians: you learn this quick-
> est and most persuasively by putting the 'Methodist Hymnal'
> alongside the 'Worshipbook' (1972). Or you should be able to.[10]

A hymn can change its meaning according to the occasion
on which it is sung. The hymn 'The Day Thou Gavest, Lord,
is Ended' was originally written in 1870 for a liturgy for
missionary meetings. In 1897 Queen Victoria chose it for her
Diamond Jubilee celebrations when it was sung at thousands
of churches throughout the land on Sunday 20 June of that
year. It is frequently used now at the funeral services of the
elderly. It is obvious that it has meant something different on
all these occasions. A change of meaning can also be brought
about by an editor or compiler who wields considerable power.
Isaac Watts' 'Our God, our help in ages past' (based on psalm
90) was arguably composed when the sudden death of Queen

Anne removed the threat of further discrimination against the Dissenters. It was changed to 'O God, our help in ages past' by John Wesley who felt that a broader community than the 'gathered church' for which it was written would benefit from it. By the late nineteenth century it became almost a tribal chant of the English, sung on national occasions. This same hymn has consoled the mourning family with assurances of immortality and it has assured the British that their one thousand year monarchy would continue. The addition or subtraction of a verse or even a line can change the meaning of the most well-known hymn in order to adapt it to the editor's theological or devotional view-point. 'For the Beauty of the Earth' was written about 1863 by Folliott Sandford Pierpoint and was meant to be sung at Holy Communion, originally being published in a collection called *Lyra Eucharistica*. The original chorus to be sung at the end of each verse was:

> Christ our God, to Thee we raise
> This our sacrifice of praise.

Some editors wanted to make this hymn available at times other than at Holy Communion while explicitly naming Christ as God and linking sacrifice with the Eucharist was not acceptable to other editors. The 1904 edition of *Hymns Ancient and Modern* placing it under the section of 'General Hymns', omits some of the verses and alters the chorus to:

> Lord of all, to Thee we raise
> This our grateful hymn of praise.

Songs of Praise also includes it in the 'General' section and with the book's stress on character and intelligence ensures that the verse (omitted by *Hymns Ancient and Modern*) which states this preference is included:

> For the joy of ear and eye,
> For the heart and brain's delight,
> For the mystic harmony
> Linking sense to sound and sight.

In accordance with its theological preference of the relationship to the Father, the chorus is again changed to

> Father, unto thee we raise
> This our sacrifice of praise.

English Hymnal (1906) and its successor *New English Hymnal* (1986) retain the words and position of the original, reflecting their Catholic understanding of the Holy Communion and their 'high' Christology. *The Baptist Hymn Book* (1962) locates it under the heading of 'Worship and Praise' changing the chorus yet again to

> Christ, our Lord, to Thee we raise
> This our hymn of grateful praise.

The Baptist Hymn Book's successor, *Baptist Praise and Worship* (1991) places the hymn under 'Creation and Providence' and wanting to emphasize the creator uses the refrain:

> Father, unto you we raise
> this our sacrifice of praise.

The Congregational Hymnal (1951) publishes the hymn under 'The Eternal Father – His Works in Creation' and uses the same chorus as *Songs of Praise*, though omitting the verse that *Songs of Praise* felt it important to include. However, *Rejoice and Sing* (1991), the successor to *The Congregational Hymnal*, retains the verse so important to *Songs of Praise*, substituting 'mind' for 'brain' and locates the hymn under 'All God's Created Works', but provides yet another version of the chorus:

> Gracious God to thee we raise
> this our sacrifice of praise.

It is impossible to think of a hymn without thinking of its tune. Many people can sing a hymn tune perfectly but will stumble over the words. Just as the words of hymns resonate with contemporary culture, so do the tunes to which the words are sung. Music defines one community over and against another; in a similar way, the tunes to which hymns are sung are making a statement about how the Church defines itself. For example, hymns that are sung to traditional folk tunes, like the Iona hymns, are making theological statements about God at work in culture. Hymns that are sung to plainsong may be perceived as

making the theological statement that the God who has always been
at work in creation is still at work, or they may be perceived as
saying that the God who is being praised is remote from the world
which the Church regards as beyond the redemption of God.

It is something about the marriage of tune and words that
makes a hymn popular. Authors express in their words what
composers express in their music. When souls meet in this way
and find that they are expressing what is commonly held, then
a hymn becomes popular. We have already seen how the words
of 'Abide With Me' came to be written. According to the
widow of W. H. Monk, composer of the tune 'Eventide' to
which the hymn is sung:

> 'Abide with me' was written at a time of great sorrow. Hand in
> hand we were silently watching the glory of the setting sun (our
> daily habit) until the golden hue had faded . . . then he took
> paper and pencilled the tune which has gone over all the world.[11]

It is the tune which brings alive the words and enables them to
burrow deep into the soul.

Hymns, at their best, are, as St Augustine wrote, singing
with the praise of God, but we do not sing out of a theological,
cultural or social vacuum. Concentrating on the 'hymn explosion'
of the last thirty years, when the output of new hymns and hymnals
must be compared to the phenomenal period between 1830 and
1880 with the Church of England producing above an average of
one hymnal each year, the following chapters will be examining
the theology of hymns and the influences that shape them. It is
clear that hymns are vignettes of theology which exert an incredible amount of power and influence. Hitherto it has tended
to be the leaders of the churches (clergy, professional theologians and musicians) who have controlled this valuable resource.
What would happen if the people in the pews had a greater say
over the hymns? We shall also be considering this question.

It was the nineteenth-century Congregationalist minister
R. W. Dale who recognized the power and potential of hymns
when he wrote:

> Let me write the hymns of a Church and I care not who writes
> the theology.[12]

2

Hymns and Theology

All theologies are contextually conditioned. There is nothing wrong with theology being contextually conditioned. It may take others to show us how conditioned or ideologically captive our own theology is. Even if once we could ignore such voices, now we can no longer do so.

Charles Kraft

The task of theology is to make sense of life, with all its paradoxes and ambiguities, in the light of the reality of God. One of the major contributions of theology in the third world is to show how all theology is contextual. To put it another way, theology comes from concrete situations and addresses specific needs. Thus, Liberation Theology arose in the context of the dispossessed of South America struggling to discover what the Gospel was saying in their specific situation. Minjung Theology arose in Korea where the people felt that they needed their voice to be heard and acknowledged. Black Theology arose in North America because Blacks did not feel that American white theology acknowledged the sufferings of Black people who could not identify with traditional theological thought forms. All these theologies are clearly contextual. But it is easy to forget that the traditional theologies which Christians have tended to regard as true and immutable for all people for all time are also contextual. Let us consider some examples.

Psalm 137 is the lament of the people of Israel held captive in Babylon in the sixth century before Christ. Their feelings of desperation and resentment become most apparent in the last stanza:

By the streams of Babylon
we sat and wept
at the memory of Zion
leaving our harps
hanging on the poplars there.

For we had been asked
to sing to our captors,
to entertain those who had carried us off:
'Sing' they said
'some hymns of Zion'.

How could we sing
one of Yahweh's hymns
in a pagan country?
Jerusalem, if I forget you,
may my right hand wither!

May I never speak again
if I forget you!
If I do not count Jerusalem
the greatest of my joys!

Yahweh, remember what the Sons of Edom did
on the day of Jerusalem,
how they said, 'Down with her!
Raze her to the ground!'

Destructive daughter of Babel,
a blessing on the man who treats you
as you have treated us,
a blessing on him who takes and dashes
your babies against the rock!

The feelings of depression, as expressed in this psalm, brought
on by being unable to sing about God (Yahweh) when exiled
from where the heart feels most at home (in this case,
Jerusalem), may well speak to the experience and knowledge
of many people, but they arose from a specific context and will

speak most powerfully to people who find themselves in similar circumstances to the psalmist.

Old Testament scholars are generally agreed that the first five books of the Bible, the Pentateuch, were compiled when the Israelites were in exile in Babylon in the sixth century before Christ. The exiled Israelites would have been comforted, reassured and inspired as they heard about the promise of posterity and land which God had made to Abraham and which they would inherit. They would have been chastened to hear how human initiatives apart from God ultimately lead to failure and they would have been encouraged to hear how God corrects his people but does not abandon them. As we reflect today on these insights into God and his relationship with humanity, we need to remember that this theology was formulated in a specific context to address a particular situation.

In the New Testament, different understandings of Jesus Christ (different theologies) are revealed as the gospel writers adapt their message to be received by different people living and working in different circumstances. In St Mark is seen an enigmatic Jesus who spends much of his time working in and on the edge of society (his ministry begins in Galilee and only at the end does he enter Jerusalem). Many of his miracles are performed quietly when he asks that nobody should be told of them:

> Jesus . . . sent him [the healed leper] away and sternly ordered him, 'Mind you say nothing to anyone' (1.44),

and his death is agonizing:

> And at the ninth hour Jesus cried in a loud voice, 'Eloi, Eloi, lama sabachthani?' which means 'My God, my God, why have you deserted me?' . . . Jesus gave a loud cry and breathed his last (15.33–7).

At the centre of the gospel Jesus asks his followers who they think he is:

> Who do people say I am? (8.27–30)

and even by the end of the gospel his identity is never completely revealed, but the reader is encouraged to continue his own search:

> He is going before you to Galilee; it is there you will see him, just as he told you (16.7–8).

By contrast, St John tells his readers precisely who Jesus is:

> In the beginning was the Word: the Word was with God and the Word was God (1.1).

And very quickly Jesus is making his presence felt in Jerusalem:

> Making a whip out of some chord, he drove them all [money changers and traders] out of the Temple . . . 'Take all of this out of here and stop turning my Father's house into a market' (2.15–16).

Jesus' miracles are public and often controversial and his death is more akin to the gentle finishing of a task (his final words are, 'It is accomplished') than to a cry of desolation. Some people find that the theology of St Mark's Gospel speaks powerfully to them, whereas others have a preference for St John: it could be that such preference is dictated by an identification with the context in which the gospels were written.

The letters of St Paul are particularly clear examples of the fact that all theology is contextual. The letters reveal young churches struggling to make the Gospel real and alive for them. The first letter to the Corinthians (especially chapters 12 to 14) shows different groups within the Church struggling to 'contextualize' even further by making the Gospel not only real to the Church community in Corinth, but also to the various and influential freemen, like Titus Justus and Gaius, in whose houses Christians gathered for worship. There were also uneducated slaves and dock-workers who made up the largest group (Chloe seems to have been their leader). There were educated slaves, secretary slaves and house slaves who worked for the Roman administration. There were also women. Not surprisingly, conflicts arose among and between these different groupings about the desired form of worship – some wanted to be spontaneous and charismatic, while others wanted more tradition, control and intelligibility – and the conduct of different groups. Out of these difficult circumstances comes the famous Pauline passage on how the body works (I Cor 12.4–30) and how love is needed to sustain such a community (I Cor 13.1–13).[1]

The fact that theology is contextual is also apparent in the Church's creeds. Phrases like, 'eternally begotten of the Father, Light from Light, true God from true God, begotten not made, of one Being with the Father . . . he became incarnate of the Virgin Mary' from the Nicene Creed hark back to a former age and former debates. The formation of the creeds shows a predominantly Greek Church struggling, in their language and thought forms, to make sense of a faith that had Jewish origins.

When the way that theology is expressed no longer speaks to people, then the time has come to formulate it afresh in words and symbols that are meaningful. That is what contextualizing is all about. Liberation Theology, Minjung theology and Black Theology, with which this chapter began, are continuing the tradition of contextualization which can be traced back to the Old Testament.

Hymns are contextual theology in that they have emerged from specific contexts. 'All Creatures of our God and King', for example, is based on 'Canticle of the Sun' composed over a period of time by St Francis of Assisi who, at the age of twenty-five years, renounced all his many earthly possessions and 'wedded Lady Poverty'. The first four verses, praising the creation which Francis loved so much, probably came to the saint after a forty-day vigil in his hut at San Damiano. The reference to fire in the third verse –

> Thou fire so masterful and bright,
> that givest man both warmth and light . . .

– is said to be linked with the time when Francis was in danger of going blind. Before cauterizing his eyes without an anaesthetic he said:

> Brother Fire, God made you beautiful and strong and useful.
> I pray you to be courteous to me.

The fifth verse –

> And all ye men of tender heart,
> forgiving others, take your part . . .
> Ye who long pain and sorrow bear,
> praise God and on him cast your care . . .

– is said to have been added after a quarrel between the local
magistrates and the Bishop of Assisi. The reference to pain may
well refer to one of the illnesses that Francis had to bear. The
sixth verse –

> And thou, most kind and gentle death,
> waiting to hush our latest breath . . .
> Thou leadest home the child of God,
> And Christ our Lord the way hath trod . . .

– was written when Francis, in great pain and nearly blind, had
a vision that his own earthly sufferings were near their end. All
the verses are wrapped around with an insight into a God who
is cosmic yet personal.

Sometimes events in Scripture are used to convey or intro-
duce the hymn-writer's message, which may come from a totally
different but none the less specific context. 'Now Thank We
All Our God' is based on Ecclesiasticus 50.22–3:

> And now bless the God of all things, the doer of great deeds
> everywhere, who has exalted our days from the womb and
> acted towards us in his mercy. May he grant us cheerful heart
> and bring peace in our time, in Israel for ages on ages.

The hymn began its life as a German grace which was written
350 years ago to be sung after meals in the difficult days of the
Thirty Years War. The author, Martin Rinkart, was appointed
pastor in his native village of Eilenburg in 1617 and he was
there while his parishes were subjected to the ravages of the
war. In addition to this, the village was struck by plague in
1687 when over 8,000 inhabitants died, Rinkart himself bury-
ing 4,000 of them. While the plague was ravaging Eilenburg,
the Swedish army occupied the village and demanded a large
tribute which Rinkart managed to reduce. 'Now Thank We All
Our God' was allegedly written in the midst of these dire

circumstances and singing it would have evoked a similar kind
of hope to that given to the Israelites when they heard the
reading of the Pentateuch in exile.[2] The hymn is a reminder of
how God has been loving and gracious in the past and prays
that he may be so in the present:

> Now thank we all our God,
> with heart and hand and voices,
> Who wondrous things hath done
> In whom his world rejoices;
> Who from our mother's arms
> Hath blessed us on our way
> With countless gifts of love,
> And still is ours today.
>
> O may this bounteous God
> Through all our life be near us,
> With ever joyful hearts
> And blessed peace to cheer us;
> And keep us in his grace,
> And guide us when perplexed,
> And free us from all ills
> In this world and the next.

Theology is also partisan – and necessarily so. Psalm 137
would have brought comfort to its author and those who identified with his position: it would not have brought comfort to
those enemies whom he wanted killed. The Pentateuch may
have brought comfort and inspiration to the exiled Israelites,
but its consequent building of the Israelites' confidence and
self-image would have been potentially subversive for the Baby-
lonians who were keeping the Israelites away from their beloved
homeland. So too the struggle revealed in the first letter to
the Corinthians reveals various groupings within the Church
objecting to theology being expressed only in one way which
would exclude others.

The story behind the creeds reveals how power politics linked
with the need for theology to be partisan provides a potentially
explosive mixture. For example, behind the Nicene Creed (325
AD) was the primary theological issue of the relationship

between God the Father and the Son, but inextricably linked
with this was the political issue as to which bishopric was
the most powerful in the Church. By opting for a particular
understanding of Christ and the Trinity, the Church was deliberately excluding some people. As Church historian Diarmid
MacCulloch comments:

> Theology, always hotly debated in church circles, was now
> often decided in circumstances which remind one more of Al
> Capone's Chicago than the shores of the Sea of Galilee.[3]

The partisan nature of theology is a strength – since it speaks
directly to people's real situations – but it can also exclude
people both by accident, and, as with the creeds, by design.
Hymns can also be partisan in nature. In Chapter 1 we saw
how the hymn 'Forth in thy Name, O Lord, I Go' appealed to
a university-educated clergyman in a way that it would not
to farm labourers. In a similar fashion, the Taizé chant,

> How blest are those who are poor,
> The Kingdom of God is theirs,

would have an attraction to a congregation which considered
itself poor but not to one that knew it was rich.

It is not only what theology is actually saying that is contextual, but also the way in which it is being said. Theology is
frequently being expressed through narrative, dreams, song,
liturgy, parables, miracles, credal formulations, in systematic
form and through pastoral practice. The context in which
theology is being communicated dictates its form. So, for the
dispirited Israelites in exile in Babylon needing to hear how
God created them and how he continues to love them, the
narrative of the creation stories was an effective way of speaking
to them. It was through the medium of song that they could
best express their desolation (Psalm 137). Jesus Christ showed
the mystery of God's Kingdom by addressing his predominantly
non-literate hearers in parables and the gospel writers found
that the miracles with which their readers would have been
familiar were another medium for communicating theology.
Academics use the lecture hall, the book and the article to
communicate to students and fellow academics and systematic

theology has been considered the form which most easily lends itself to this kind of communication. When the people of God are gathered for worship, the prayer and the hymn are the communal way of expressing theology. These are all different ways of communicating. The problem is that some people maintain that some ways (often the ways with which they feel most comfortable) of communicating theology are better than others, thereby implying that other ways are inferior. Desmond Tutu, addressing other Africans, criticizes this tendency, pointing out that trying to communicate in a medium which is not natural inhibits authentic theological thought and exploration:

> We are still too concerned to play the game according to the white man's rules when he often is the referee as well. Why should we feel embarrassed if our theology is not systematic? Why should we feel that something is amiss if our theology is too dramatic for verbalisation but can be expressed only adequately in the joyous song and the scintillating movement of Africa's dance in the liturgy? Let us develop our insights about the corporateness of human existence in the face of excessive western individualism, about the wholeness of the person when others are concerned for Hellenistic dichotomies of soul and body, about the reality of the spiritual when others are made desolate with the poverty of the material. Let African Theology enthuse about the awesomeness of the transcendent when others are embarrassed to speak about the King, high and lifted up, whose train fills the Temple. It is only when African theology is true to itself that it will go on to speak relevantly to the contemporary African – surely its primary task – and also, incidentally, make its valuable contribution to the rich Christian heritage which belongs to all of us.[4]

Theology is true to its vocation when it encourages the Christian community to participate actively in the life to which it gives verbal formulation. It can only begin to do this if it speaks to the heart of the people both in the issues it addresses and in the way it addresses them.

There are, then, many ways of communicating and expressing theology; none is superior to any other, but all need each other. Walter Hollenweger, formerly Professor of Mission at the University of Birmingham, combining his great breadth of experience of the worldwide church with his formidable skills as a systematic theologian, has redefined the relationship between these different expressions of theology under the heading of Intercultural Theology, whose task is:

> the search for a 'body of Christ' theology in which each organ remains true to its function and purpose but at the same time contributes to the whole body without assuming that it is the most important, the most theological or the most academic member of that body.[5]

Hymns are valid expressions of theology both within and outside the liturgy. Like other expressions of theology, such as propositional theology, pastoral theology and liturgy, they need to be tested and challenged within the Christian community. We need to ask whether the message of the hymn and the way in which it is communicating that message can be coherently explained or acted upon or prayed. If a hymn appears to have no theology at all, what purpose does it fulfil in the context in which it is being sung? Does it enable the community to have a deeper relationship with God, within itself, with the world? Does it add another dimension to faith? Hymns can bring challenges which require careful examination before there is any attempt to reject them.

We have already seen how hymns, as Christian folksongs, relate to the cultural and social background from which they come. This relationship between hymns and culture is an indicator of the relationship between theology and culture which has been the subject of much debate. Christianity is a faith which is at the same time both incarnational,

> The Word was made flesh, he lived among us (John 1.4),

and yet is not limited by the world, making some view the world as a place to be tolerated or even dismissed:

> If you belonged to the world, the world would love you as its own; but because you do not belong to the world, because my choice withdrew you from the world, therefore the world hates you (John 15.19).

Throughout its 2,000-year history Christianity has struggled with this tension. At times Christians have embraced the world, often compromising their faith, and at other times they have gone to the other extreme and rejected the world, ignoring God's activity in it. It is significant that it was when the Church became an accepted and powerful force in the world, in the fourth century, that a group of men and women turned their backs on the world and went to find God in the silence and solitude of the desert, thereby beginning the monastic movement.

Today, too, there are groups of Christians who feel that the main-line Churches have become so much a part of the world that they have lost their cutting edge. In order that the 'purity' of the faith may be retained, those in the former group have withdrawn from the world as much as possible since they believe that the world is tainted with sin and beyond saving. Both attitudes can be found in hymns. In John Arlott's hymn, 'God, whose Farm is All Creation' the world reflects God's glory as worshippers are encouraged to offer all of life to God – hopes and fears, thinking, planning and waiting, labour and watching, with the final lines:

> in these crops of your creation,
> take, O God: they are our prayer.[6]

An example of a group reflecting this feeling that the world is tainted and Christians who are part of it compromised in some way is to be found in the hymns written by young people of the Anglican Church of the Zambian Copperbelt township of Kasompe. This township is on the outskirts of the mining town of Chingola and the writers are concerned that their elders have too easily identified Western, worldly standards of success as the standards of Christ. Being dressed in smart, clean clothes and wearing a tie is the privilege of the few in some Zambian townships and the following verses comment on its significance. The hymn was written in the vernacular (ci-Bemba) and the translation is as close to the original as possible:

1   When the sun rises I put on clean clothes thinking I'm
    of forever. I'm the walking death.

Chorus: Jesus is the glory, has the power to overcome death
on his cross. Jesus, his glory.

2   When I put on properly I cheat myself. I put on a tie, I
    think I'm forever. I'm a walking death.[7]

Whether the Christian faith is world-affirming or world-deny-
ing, whether the faith is being expressed by a community which
wishes to show acceptance or denial of the world, the language
and thought forms must make sense in the society in which
they are being used. So references to farms, crops, hopes, fears,
thinking, planning, waiting, labour and watching and the way
that these aspects of life are linked will be understandable to
those for whom Arlott writes in the same way that wearing
clean clothes and a tie makes sense to the church members of
Kasompe township. The way in which theology and society
interact is a question for debate; the fact that they do interact
is beyond dispute. In addition, the language used to express
the theology will determine how and by whom it will be
received. This is especially an issue today as the debate continues as to whether God should be addressed exclusively in
male terms. Robin Scroggs, Professor of New Testament at
Chicago Theological Seminary endorses these points when he
writes,

> What is potentially threatening is that language, including theo-
> logical language, is never to be seen as independent of other
> social realities. Thus theological language and the claims made
> therein can no longer be explained without taking into account
> socioeconomic-cultural factors as essential ingredients in the
> production of that language.[8]

Theology and society also interact at a more dynamic level,
as can be seen in the way that social conditions can favour the
emphasis of one particular doctrine in preference to another.
Such emphases have been happening throughout the history of
Christianity. It was the poverty of the peasantry in the face
of the growing wealth of the middle classes and urban prole-
tariat in Latin America that was the seed-bed for Liberation
Theology in the 1970s. Doctrines favouring liberation and free-

dom are preferred by Liberation Theologians as can be seen
from the biblical books favoured by Liberation Theology,
namely Exodus (with its emphasis on the freeing of a mass of
slaves who became the people of God), the prophets (with
their uncompromising defence of the liberator God and their
vigorous denunciation of injustices and support of the poor,
the fatherless and the widows), the gospels (with their
centrality of the divine person of Jesus, his announcement of
the Kingdom and his death and resurrection), the Acts of the
Apostles (with their portrayal of a free and liberating
community) and the Book of Revelation (with its description
of the immense struggles of the people of God against all the
monsters of history).[9] Their hymns also reflect their theological preferences as can be seen from this processional
song from the 'Misa Popular Nicaraguense' with its references
to the 'powerless', 'hungry', 'poor' and 'desperate' and the
conviction that 'Christ is stronger than the strength of sin or
sword':

> For the world and all its people
> we address our prayers to God.
>
> *Chorus*: Confidently, all can worship
> in the presence of the Lord.
>
> All the powerless, all the hungry
> are most precious to their God.
>
> For the poor, God has a purpose,
> for the desperate, a word.
>
> Christ is here and Christ is stronger
> than the strength of sin or sword.
>
> God will fill the earth with justice
> when our will and his accord.[10]

In Zambia where, compared with Latin America, the Christian faith is a recent arrival, people are facing an identity crisis. The authority of the tribe, though still strong, is being questioned as the 'nation' is being emphasized as the centre of loyalty. In addition to this, Western-style influence and power are more available to more Zambians. Accordingly, the emphasis is on incarnational theology. The questions being asked are Christological: who is Christ, is he a great ancestor or is he different? How does Christ relate to God the Creator? The following hymn speaks of heaven as a great city where Jesus is the head. God the Father is not mentioned, perhaps because those who die (the ancestors) do not traditionally enter into God's presence; hence there are unanswered questions of the relationship between Jesus and his Father and precisely who Jesus is:

> And Jesus is the head of that City which is beautiful,
> We shall sing and say hosanna when reaching heaven,
> We shall be happy for ever.[11]

In the middle of the last century, wealth and progress were prominent features of Victorian England. At this time, the up-and-coming middle classes were establishing themselves and the urban working classes were convinced that they were as marginalized in the cities as they were in the rural areas. These changes in self-understanding were reflected in the doctrines that were emphasized. There was, for example, a preference for the immortality of the soul rather than the resurrection of the body in the Victorian understanding of the afterlife. Throughout the history of Christianity, both doctrines have been held, and at different times one or the other has been prominent.[12] The Victorians favoured the immortality of the soul since it spoke of the afterlife beginning immediately after death (there was no long sleep awaiting the Last Judgement) and fitted in well with the progress that was so much a feature of their society. Victorians saw themselves as 'in via', on the way, rather than in possession, and this is reflected by the popularity of hymns on the theme of pilgrimage:

> Guide me, O thou great Redeemer,
> Pilgrim through this barren land;

I am weak, but thou art mighty,
Hold me with thy powerful hand;
Bread of heaven
Feed me now and evermore.

O happy band of pilgrims,
If onward ye will tread
With Jesus as your Fellow
To Jesus as your Head!

The following hymn also reflects the Victorian concern for wealth as the hymn-writer describes the temptations faced on earth as jewels, powerful symbols of wealth:

What are they but his jewels
Of right celestial worth?
What are they but the ladder
Set up to heav'n on earth?

Both these hymns are found in the 1861 version of *Hymns Ancient and Modern*.

Hymns may also make social or political comments by the way in which theological statements are juxtaposed. The most frequently quoted example of this is in the hymn 'All Things Bright and Beautiful', where verse 3 reads:

The rich man in his castle,
The poor man at his gate,
God made them, high or lowly,
And order'd their estate.

Mrs Alexander, the author, is endorsing the political status quo and, by enabling such words to be sung in church, is giving it a divine sanction. But such endorsement of the status quo can be more subtle, as in the hymn, 'My God, How Wonderful Thou Art'. This hymn has a very high view of God –

How dread are thine eternal years,
O everlasting Lord,
By prostrate spirits day and night
Incessantly adored!

– a very low view of humanity and a strong sense of sin:

> Oh how I fear Thee, living God,
> With deepest, tenderest fears,
> And worship thee with trembling hope,
> And penitential tears
>
> . . .
>
> For thou hast stoop'd to ask of me
> The love of my poor heart
>
> No earthly father loves like thee,
> No mother, e'er so mild,
> Bears and forbears as thou hast done
> With me thy sinful child.
>
> Father of Jesus, love's reward,
> What rapture will it be,
> Prostrate before thy throne to lie,
> And gaze and gaze on thee.

This hymn contains some classical theological statements, but the way in which they have been combined encourages the singer to have a low self-opinion in the face of God who is overbearing yet benign and whose authority and power are absolute. The attitude towards self and authority which is encouraged within the Church will usually be duplicated outside the Church and so churchgoers will be encouraged to react in a similar way to all authority figures.

Again, third world theologians have reminded Western theologians that there has always been a social dynamic in theology (frequently with a bias towards those in power) but either it has not been recognized or it has been ignored. Theology can never be reduced to a purely social dynamic, making God into a supernatural glue to keep people together within society and culture, but without an awareness of this dynamic, theology can be a form of manipulation. All theology is contextual, using words and images that express reality in terms that may be acceptable to some people but not to others. Hymns are no less partisan and need to be looked at and sung in an arena which is both affirming and challenging. But to deny the value

of hymns as valid expressions of theology is to deny a voice to
the group which constitute the largest part of our congregations.

3

From Psalmody to Negro Spirituals

We were baptised and all anxiety over the past melted away from us. The days were all too short, for I was lost in wonder and joy, meditating upon your far-reaching providence for the salvation of the human race. The tears flowed from me when I heard your hymns and canticles, for the sweet singing of your Church moved me deeply. The music surged in my ears, truth seeped into my heart, and my feelings of devotion overflowed, so that tears streamed down. But they were tears of gladness.

St Augustine

In order to understand how hymns have reached the form we have today it is necessary to consider the roots. When we do of hymns consider such roots we also become aware of the potential of hymns which, for various reasons, has not been realized. In these next two chapters we shall be considering the development of hymns, their theological function and their relationship with their culture from psalmody to the hymnody of the First World War. The treatment here is not a systematic historical survey but a highlighting of certain movements relevant to the overall theme of this book.

The greatest influence on the formation of hymns is the psalter. Psalms have been a major way in which the Old Testament has permeated the Church and, like hymns, psalms are known in circles far wider than the Church. Although they may be less common to churchgoers whose only diet is the Parish Communion, they nevertheless will be encountered by many (churchgoers and non-churchgoers alike) at weddings and funerals. Indeed, up until the beginning of the nineteenth century, they were the only songs allowed to be sung in the

Church of England and there are still churches, in particular in some areas of Scotland, where the psalm paraphrases provide the sole musical diet. Many of the great Christian teachers (for example, Origen, Chrysostom, Augustine, Thomas Aquinas) have given a great deal of their energies to expounding the psalms.

Many people experience psalms today through saying them, hearing them sung by a choir, struggling through Anglican Chant, singing one of the paraphrases ('The Lord's my Shepherd', 'O God Our Help in Ages Past') or joining in the contemporary antiphonal chants of composers like Gelineau and Dom Gregory Murray. None of these methods reproduces the dramatic and colourful way in which they would have been used by the ancient Israelites.

Scholars have become increasingly aware of the importance of the 'cult' in Old Testament times. The cult is the complex of festivals, customs, sacrifices and prophecy that made up the public performance of worship. The festivals (in particular the Passover, Festival of Weeks and Tabernacles) were the most important times of the year and through them the central stories, laws and traditions were linked with the formation of the distinctive identity of Israel. The formation of the monarchy under Saul, David and Solomon brought changes in the cult, especially with the building of the Temple in Jerusalem and the involvement of the king in the ceremonies and festivals. Most of the psalms were composed at this creative period of Israel's worship. During these festivals there were, at various points, acts of purification, dramas of God's victory over his enemies and his testing and support of the king. There were also recitals of significant parts of the Covenant and sacrifices which expressed central aspects of the Covenant worship such as praise and thanksgiving, atonement and reconciliation. Worshippers were involved physically in washing, shouting, prostrating, dancing, clapping, singing and feasting. The psalms sprang from this vivid, multi-layered worship, articulating and lifting up all these things to God. So, for example, Psalm 96 welcomes God (Yahweh) as he comes among worshippers in power, salvation and judgement:

> Sing Yahweh a new song!
> Sing to Yahweh, all the earth!
> Sing to Yahweh, bless his name.
>
> Proclaim his salvation day after day,
> tell of his glory among the nations,
> tell his marvels to every people . . .
>
> Let the heavens be glad, let earth rejoice,
> let the sea thunder and all that it holds,
> let the fields exult and all that is in them,
> let all the woodland trees cry out for joy,
>
> at the presence of Yahweh for he comes,
> he comes to judge the earth,
> to judge the world with justice
> and the nations with his truth.

And Psalm 20 is an appeal for support of the king:

> May Yahweh answer you in time of trouble,
> may the name of the God of Jacob protect you!
>
> May he send you help from the sanctuary,
> give you support from Zion,
> remember all your oblations
> and find your holocausts acceptable;
> may he grant you your heart's desire,
> and crown all your plans with success . . .
>
> Yahweh, save the king,
> answer us when we call.

The psalms are also full of prophecies showing how dramatic, prophetic interaction between God and Israel were part of worship. Prophets spoke on behalf of God as well as on behalf of the people in intercession as in Psalm 50:

> Listen, my people, I am speaking;
> Israel, I am giving evidence against you!

> I charge, I indict you to your face,
> I, God, your God . . .
>
> You sit there, slandering your own brother,
> you malign your own mother's son.
> You do this, and expect me to say nothing?
> Do you really think I am like you?

The importance of these sentiments is that they stress the independence of God from the cult, pointing out God's holiness and sovereignty and they prevent the cult from taming God. This also shows how hymns can be vehicles of criticism towards the community as well as of praise of God. Ancient Israel's prophets exposed injustice and the violation of human dignity and linked them with a wrong understanding of God. It is through offering wholehearted praise at the same time as nurturing human dignity that the most characteristic dynamics of Judeo-Christian living are created and developed. This is well illustrated in Psalm 85.10–11:

> Love and loyalty now meet,
> Righteousness and peace now embrace;
> Loyalty reaches up from earth
> And righteousness leans down from heaven.

We shall see below how this linkage is also particularly strong in the Negro Spirituals.

The psalms thus captured a great deal of the atmosphere and excitement of what happened at these festivals, and later recitation, whether in the agonizing separation from their beloved Israel in exile or in the more sober atmosphere of the synagogue, would have transported the hearers back to the context in which they were written and on to the God whom they were praising. This contact with the past would ideally have renewed and reinvigorated the hearers for their present and future. The psalms, then, set a pattern for praise and worship which continues to exercise great influence over the Church. Churches frequently regard the psalms as touchstones for musical revision, but too often the dynamic worship in which the psalms were set and the dramatic way in which they were frequently used are forgotten as an appeal to the psalms becomes an appeal to conservatism.

We need to turn to the Church in the East to see the appearance of the non-biblical hymn. Originally there was a clear reluctance to allow into worship anything that was not based on the Bible, yet the Church was forced to use hymns because of their popular appeal and in order to fight against heretical influences. In Syria in the second century, Bardaisan, a native of Edessa, propounded and popularized heretical views through the medium of hymns. The Church was forced to respond by writing hymns filled with orthodox understandings. It was Ephraim the Syrian who was at the climax of this response in the fourth century. The example of Ephraim was carried on by other writers who contributed to form a large body of Syrian hymnody.

A similar incident took place in another of the great centres of the Eastern Church. In the Church in Alexandria, Arius was preaching what the Church regarded as heresy concerning the humanity and divinity of Christ. His views were formally condemned by the Church at the Council of Nicaea (326 AD) but again they had been popularized in hymns. Hymns presenting the orthodox faith in opposition to that of the heretics were sanctioned by the Church. These hymns were doxological in character, that is they glorified the Blessed Trinity. The doxology at the end of hymns originates from these disputes and ensures that the doctrine transmitted in the hymns is orthodox. Thus hymns, which were popular in character, were used as vehicles of theology.

Before leaving the East to concentrate on how hymns became accepted in the West, it is important to be aware of the difference between hymns of the East and hymns of the West. In fact, hymns in East and West are unlike each other in most ways (scope, subject matter, metre, length) except that all alike are meant for liturgical use. Eastern hymns, which appear in many different forms, are grouped under distinctive titles such as Ode, Canon and Kontakion, according to their liturgical use and characteristic structure. Often translations into English make them appear very similar to the Western type upon which the English hymn as we know it is based.

The earliest hymn-writing in the West also began under the influence of the Arian controversy. Hilary of Poitiers (known as the 'Hammer of the Arians') was forced from his diocese in 356 to Phrygia as a result of the struggle between Orthodox and Arian and spent six years in surroundings where hymns were probably in common use. On his return he wrote the first essay on Latin hymnody and composed some hymns. However, it was Ambrose, appointed bishop of Milan in 374, who is known as the father of Church song. Like Hilary he had spent time in the East and brought back with him new ideas to Milan. Again like Hilary he was forced to confront the Arian controversy and it was such a confrontation with an Arian empress in 386 that first called out his powers as a hymn-writer. St Augustine, a disciple of Ambrose describes the confrontation in his *Confessions*:

> Justina, the mother of the boy emperor Valentinian, had been persecuting your devoted servant Ambrose in the interests of the heresy into which the Arians had seduced her. In those days your faithful people used to keep watch in the church, ready to die with their bishop, your servant. My mother, your handmaid, was there with them, taking a leading part in that anxious time of vigilance and living a life of constant prayer. Although I was not yet fired by the warmth of your Spirit, these were stirring times for me as well, for the city was in a state of alarm and excitement. It was then that the practice of singing hymns and psalms was introduced, in keeping with the usage of the Eastern churches, to revive the flagging spirits of the people during their long and cheerless watch. Ever since then the custom has been retained, and the example of Milan has been followed in many other places, in fact in almost every church throughout the world.[1]

One can never be absolutely certain that hymns attributed to these earliest writers are their actual composition, but it is extremely likely, not least because Augustine himself bears witness to it, that Ambrose composed the hymn from which the following is extracted. Note the emphasis on the identity of Christ (which was at the heart of the Arian controversy) and the doxology at the end:

O come, Redeemer of the earth,
Show to the world Thy virgin birth;
Let age to age the wonder tell;
Such birth, O God, beseems Thee well.

No earthly father dost Thou own;
By God's o'ershadowing alone
The Word made flesh to man is come,
The fair fruit of a mother's womb . . .

From God the Father He proceeds,
To God the Father back He speeds;
Runs out His course to death and hell,
Returns on God's high throne to dwell.

O ancient as the Father Thou,
Gird on our flesh for victory now;
the weakness of our mortal state
With deathless might invigorate . . .

All praise to God the Father be,
All praise, Eternal Son, to Thee,
Whom with the Spirit we adore,
For ever and for evermore.[2]

We can see how hymns, in their earliest times, have had a
strong 'popular' streak to them and, because of their links with
heresy, they would have been viewed by the Church with a
certain amount of suspicion. They were, nevertheless, taken
and embraced by the Church and used regularly in religious
communities. It was the medieval religious carol that gave the
people back their voice.

The carol had its origins in dance and had strong associations
with pagan rites. For centuries the medieval Church tried to
stamp out dances and songs which were based on pagan
worship not merely because the performances were accompanied
by lewd words and gestures but also because of people's habit
of dancing on the eves of church festivals and in the precincts of
the churchyard or even within the church itself. In 1497

Laurence Wade, the monk of Christ Church, Canterbury, who translated the life of Thomas Becket into English verse, refers, in that work, to carols in the same breath as unworthy songs:

Off all maner off karolles and songes dissolute.[3]

However, it soon became clear that the carol form could not be stamped out by the Church but that it could be used to express Christian sentiments. One can see immediately the parallel between these circumstances and those of the early Church accepting the hymn form to fight against heresy. One group which was influential in the development of the English carol was the Franciscans. These wandering friars had had a similar influence in Italy and France, but it was in the fourteenth and fifteenth centuries that their presence was felt in the realm of popular religious song in England. Knowing the song of the Church themselves and encountering, through their wanderings, men and women of diverse backgrounds, they helped the creation of a religious song form which ordinary people came to sing quite naturally. Eventually the religious carol, which had been sung at different times throughout the year and had been associated with dance, came to be associated with singing at Christmas and left behind its link with dance. Christmastide was the chief occasion of dances, song and celebration and extended, with the intervening feast days, to the Epiphany. Christmas is, of course, the successor to the older pagan winter feast, hence the outbreaks of dance and song which caused a problem to the Church. This adapting of the carol for Christian use evolved over a long period. Its success was due to the fact that it enabled people to identify with the Holy Family, thereby providing a link with the more formal liturgical devotion of the Church. In the carol that follows there is a clear identification of Christ with the poor and, by taking a line or two from a Latin hymn sung in Church, a clear link between Church and people:

> Between an ox and an asse
> Enixa est puerpera;
> In pore clothing he was
> Qui regnat super ethera.[4]

Not all carols were sympathetic towards the peasantry, as those which, for instance, spoke of the humble circumstances of Christ's birth. Some were aristocratic as the references to various ranks and the requirement to bring some kind of contribution ('sport') indicate:

> Lett no man cum into this hall,
> Grome, page, nor yet marshall,
> But that sum sport he brying withall,
> For now ys the tyme of Crystmas.[5]

There are clearly some carols for the peasants (usually identified by a preoccupation with humble circumstances) and some for the nobility. The religious orders would celebrate the season with their own hymns.

The early English carol is very different from the majority of carols which are traditionally sung at Christmas. They are rarely heard today, but they are important in the development of the hymn because they illustrate how the Church has used popular culture (lower and aristocratic) to enshrine its message. Many of the carols may have been written by religious professionals (the friars) but they certainly appealed to and were sung by the wider populace. Richard Greene, who has made one of the finest compilations of early English carols, says that they may not have been 'popular in origin' (that is, written by the people who came to sing them) but they were certainly 'popular by destination' (that is, acknowledged, accepted and sung by them).[6] Another feature that is important about these carols is that they draw no sharp line between sacred and secular as indeed the people would not naturally have done themselves. The carol, then, although not allowed in Church, provided a meeting place between the people and the Church's articulation of the faith: this is an important distinction to make because it is a reminder that the Church does not often articulate the realities of the Christian faith in a language with which the majority of the population can identify.

It was the Reformation, during which hymn-singing was viewed with great suspicion in England, that was, paradoxically, significant in the development of the English hymn. Up until this time, the congregation was very much the spectator of what happened within Church since the hymns were sung in Latin by the choir. Religious lyrics sung by the congregation were only tolerated outside of the Church liturgies. But there was a new order on its way and we need to turn towards the continent to understand how it affected England. In Germany Martin Luther encouraged simple melodies familiar to ordinary people (German and Latin devotional songs, children's songs, folksongs, school songs and carols) to be used in worship – for example, the tune 'Quem Pastores Laudavere' often sung to the hymn 'Jesus Good Above All Other', and 'In Dulci Jubilo'. Words were sometimes altered or completely rewritten. Luther also wrote some hymns himself (words and melody), the most well-known being 'A Safe Stronghold our God is Still' to the tune 'Ein'feste Burg'. He was also willing to use Latin hymns of the Church. The fact that Luther drew his tunes (and sometimes the inspiration for words) from popular culture reflects his positive attitude towards culture as well as his attempts to gain wide appeal.

However, two other contemporary reformers, Zwingli and Calvin, influenced by a dualism which separated flesh from spirit or body from soul, believed that it was unacceptable for the music of the Church to be worldly: still less were songs of the Latin Church to be tolerated. It was the spirit of Calvin which pervaded the Reformation in England and Scotland and the Calvinist tradition forbade any texts to be sung in Church except the Book of Psalms and one or two canticles. In this atmosphere, the Old Metrical Version of the Psalms, known as the 'Old Version', appeared in the middle of the sixteenth century, compiled by Thomas Sternhold, assisted by John Hopkins. Sternhold's aim was to make sacred songs for the people and he wrote them in either Short Metre or Common Metre, in which three quarters of them are composed. These two metres are the most popular in hymn books today. The introduction to the 1560 version gives a valuable insight:

> Psalmes of David in Englishe metre by Thomas Sternholde and others, conferred with the Ebrue and in certeine places corrected, as the sense of the Prophete required: and the note ioyned withall. Very mete to be used of all sorts of people

privately for their Godly solace and comfort: laiying aparte all ungodly songes & ballades, which tende only to the norishing of vice and corrupting of youth. Newly set fourth and allowed according to the order appointed in the Quene's Maiestie's Iniunctions.[7]

One hymn from the 'Old Version' still frequently sung is 'All People that on Earth do Dwell' which is a version of Psalm 100.

In 1696 a completed edition of the 'New Version' of the psalms appeared under the hand of Nahum Tate (who was Poet Laureate) and Nicholas Brady. The 'New Version' never acquired the popularity of its predecessor which was still used in some places until the middle of the nineteenth century.

From a contemporary perspective, allowing the congregation to sing psalms only seems highly restrictive, but at the time this was radical: for the first time, the congregation was being given a voice in the worship of the Church. As we shall see, by having a voice in worship, the laity was being given a say in the theology and in the eventual running of the Church. Nevertheless, congregational singing must have been deplorable in some places. Nobody took psalm books to Church except the parish clerk who would lead the congregation in singing by a method known as 'lining-out'. The clerk would read out the psalm one line at a time and the congregation followed by repeating it in unison; the clerk would then proceed to the next line, the congregation would repeat that after him – and so it would continue until the end. As no musical direction was given, the singing would have been very undisciplined. It was also extremely slow: one writer tells of a vicar who, having left his sermon behind, announced a psalm, walked half a mile home and back and returned to find his congregation still singing the same psalm.[8] It was into this environment that the Dissenter Isaac Watts (1674–1748) came. He was appalled at the state of psalm-singing in churches:

> While we sing the Praises of our God in his Church, we are employ'd in that part of Worship which of all others is the nearest a-kin to Heaven; and 'tis pity that this of all others should be perform'd the worst upon Earth . . . To see the dull

Indifference, the negligent and the thoughtless Air that sits upon the Faces of the whole Assembly, while the Psalm is on their lips, might tempt even a charitable Observer to suspect the Fervency of inward Religion.[9]

Watts is an important figure in changing the direction of hymn-singing as he not only encouraged the Church to move away from its exclusive insistence on psalms, but he wrote new words to the old familiar metres, thereby making the transition gentler and less dramatic.

Hymns were being sung at the end of the seventeenth century but they were usually sung in private (Bishop Ken, for example, wrote his great hymns, 'Awake my Soul, and with the Sun' and 'Glory to Thee, my God, this Night', for scholars at Winchester College) and were regarded by some as 'popish and unscriptural'. Isaac Watts, who came to be known as the father of the English hymn, set new standards and criteria for hymns. Watts felt that psalms alone in worship were unsatisfactory because they were too close to King David and not close enough to Jesus Christ. He wrote in his Preface to his *Hymns and Spiritual Songs* (1717):

> by keeping too close to David in the House of God, the Vail of Moses is thrown over our hearts.

Watts set up a new standard of Church song with the aims that it should be 'evangelical', not in the sense that New Testament songs should be allowed to supplement the psalms but that Church song be brought within the light of the Gospel. Secondly, it should be freely composed, as against the Reformation standard of strict adherence to the letter of Scripture or the later paraphrasing of Scripture. Finally, it should express the thoughts and feelings of the singers and not merely recall the circumstances or record the sentiments of David or Asaph or anybody else. For Watts the true basis of a sympathetic devotion was not in the mind of the poet but in the thoughts, feelings and aspirations commonly held by the largest number of Christians. For a long time people had been striving to worship God in their own way: Watts gave them the means to do this. Watts did not devalue the psalms which he regarded as God's word to his people, but hymns, he believed, were the people's word to God. Watts made hymns accessible. As Bernard Manning eloquently writes:

> What of Watt's choice of subjects? What are the psalms and hymns about? They concern, as is natural, some things of passing or historic interest. In making David speak like a Christian, Watts most properly made him speak like an Englishman, not to say like an eighteenth-century Whig. Watts equates, that is to say, Palestine, Israel, Judea, Jerusalem with Great Britain. The exquisitively sensitive commentators call this vulgar. Vulgar or not, Watts does it. The result is that he gives us some fascinating reflexions on English history. The deliverances of the chosen people had parallels in the Gunpowder Plot, the landing of William of Orange, the accession of George I, and generally in the defeat of the French, the discomfiture of the Tories, and the confusion of the Papists . . . The hymns are full of sound political doctrine as well as thanksgiving.[10]

Thus the following was applied to the Glorious Revolution and King William:

> Britain was doomed to be a slave,
> Her frame dissolved, her fears were great.
> When God a new supporter gave
> To bear the pillars of the state.
>
> No vain pretence to royal birth
> Shall fix a tyrant on the throne.

And the following to Guy Fawkes, keenly felt as a Catholic plot:

> Their secret fires in caverns lay,
> And we the sacrifice;
> But gloomy caverns strove in vain
> To 'scape all searching eyes.
>
> Their dark designs were all revealed,
> Their treason all betray'd . . .

In vain the busy sons of hell
Still new rebellions try . . .

How have we chas'd them through the field,
And trod them to the ground,
While Thy salvation was our shield,
But they no shelter found . . .

In vain to idol saints they cry,
And perish in their blood.[11]

In the first part of *The Psalms of David Imitated in New Testament Language together with Hymns and Spiritual Songs*, Watts gives us the psalms of David as he believes David would have written them at the time of Christ. Two well-known hymns (psalms) from this are 'Jesus Shall Reign where e'er the Sun Does his Successive Journeys Run' (Psalm 62) and 'Our God, our Help in Ages Past' (Psalm 90). The latter is commonly sung with Wesley's change of words – 'O God, Our Help in Ages Past'. The original wording reflects Watts' contemporary concern about the place of Dissent and is a paean of rejoicing when the death of Queen Anne removed further threat against Dissenters.[12]

One of the reasons why many of Watts' hymns are not sung today is that they were written to address specific historical occasions which are no longer issues now as they were for Watts and his contemporaries. Watts was not simply referring to events of his times by juxtaposing theological symbols, but was referring to them in a direct and personal way: fellow Dissenters would immediately have recognized that he was referring to Guy Fawkes in the hymn 'Their Secret Fires in Caverns Lay' and to Queen Anne in 'Our God, our Help in Ages Past'.

Watts had the gift of using the first-person singular in his hymns, thereby making them personal while at the same time embracing the experience of many. Watts' hymns were personal without being individualistic. This gift is seen at its peak in Watts' most famous (and thought by many to be his most beautiful) hymn, 'When I Survey the Wondrous Cross', which he wrote as an exposition of Galatians 6.14. The references to the expanse of the universe, the spaciousness of nature and the vastness of time reflect the language of the great philosophical and cosmological debates of Watts' time. However, such language was unimaginable in the hymns of the people to whom we now turn, whose reputation was spreading at the end of Watts' life. In the words of L. F. Benson, author of *The English Hymn*,

> The English hymn, that had found so capable a tutor as Watts, had been waiting for so devoted a lover as Wesley.[13]

Although John Wesley probably wrote a number of hymns himself, translated many from their German originals and edited many of his brother's hymns, Charles Wesley deserves the credit as the main hymn writer. The number of hymns to come from his pen has been speculated at between 3,000 and 9,000 though more specifically 7,300 according to current scholarly opinion.[14] Charles Wesley's faith permeated the whole of his life and accordingly we even find a hymn written 'For a Child Cutting his Teeth'![15] But one of the Wesley brothers' greatest contributions to hymnody was to make it accessible to the man and woman in the pew, regardless of their background. Nineteenth-century Unitarian clergyman and philosopher James Martineau wrote in reference to the *Collection of Hymns for the Use of People called Methodists*:

> After the Scriptures, the Wesley Hymn Book appears to me the grandest instrument of popular religious culture that Christendom has ever produced.[16]

One of the appeals of the hymns was that some of their tunes took their tone from contemporary bouncy, dance-hall music. When a crew of drunken sailors loudly accompanied Wesley's preaching with their ditty 'Nancy Dawson', Charles commented that he liked their tune but not their lewd lyrics. He invited the crew to return later in the day, promising a song for them all to sing together. Expecting to make more sport of Wesley, the crew returned only to be won over to the Christian Faith by Charles' hymn 'On the True Use of Musick' which began:

> Listed into the Cause of Sin,
> Why should a Good be Evil?
> Musick, alas! too long has been
> Prest to obey the Devil:
> Drunken, or lewd, or light the Lay
> Flow'd to the Soul's Undoing,
> Widen'd, and strew'n with Flowers the Way
> Down to Eternal Ruin . . .
>
> Jesus the Soul of Musick is;
> His is the Noblest Passion:
> Jesus' Name is Joy and Peace,
> Happiness and Salvation:
> Jesus' Name the Dead can raise,
> Shew us our Sins Forgiven,
> Fill us with all the Life of Grace,
> Carry us up to Heaven.[17]

The Wesleys' Methodist Societies were founded not to replace, but to supplement the attendance of the Established Church. It was intended that the spiritual hope, growth and encouragement which was lacking in Church would be provided by the Societies. This can be seen in the book already mentioned, *A Collection of Hymns for the Use of People called Methodists*. The book, which contains some hymns from previous publications, has sections describing the pleasantness of religion, the goodness of God and the Four Last Things. There are prayers for repentance, hymns for mourners convinced of sin, for those brought to birth, for backsliders and those recovered. There are hymns for believers, rejoicing, fighting, praying, watching, working, suffering, groaning for full redemption, brought to birth, interceding for the world and for the Society. The hymns:

> are not carelessly jumbled together, but carefully arranged under proper heads, according to the experience of real Christians. So that this book is in effect a little body of experimental and practical divinity.[18]

The book was to be used as a prayer book as well as a hymn

book. However, it does not contain hymns on the great doctrines of the creed, nor those on the sacraments which shows
that at the time of its publication it was still hoped that Methodists would be welcomed to the services of the Established
Church.

One of the appeals of the Methodist Societies was the
acknowledgement and expression of emotions and feelings.
John Wesley, who had felt his heart 'strangely warmed' in the
religious experience he had at a Society meeting in Aldersgate
Street on 24 May 1738, recognized the place of emotions in
the pilgrimage of faith. Such expression, however, was neither
encouraged nor acknowledged in the Church which effectively
cut off a great number of people for whom this was the way
into faith. Many people, in particular the lower classes, experienced faith on an emotional level and, because they were
uneducated, they had no access to a language in which they
could express their faith. The Wesleys changed the atmosphere
of hymns by allowing a heightening of the emotion, new themes
and new manners of expression. They aimed many of their
hymns at the unchurched and unsaved, using song as a means of
conversion. Under Charles Wesley, hymns expressed Christian
experience as he translated every new spiritual experience into
song. Nevertheless, the Wesleys were anxious that hymn-singing
should not become an 'orgy of emotion' and so they provided
a body of authorized hymn tunes and expected no others to be
sung. Their cardinal principle in singing was that tunes should
invite the participation of all the people and keep within the
limits of sobriety and reverence. Despite all this, the hymns
were not about feelings: they acknowledged feelings but they
were not about feelings. They were primarily about Christ and
Christ crucified.

Charles Wesley's journal entry for 11 September 1748 quotes
with approval this 'charge' which the Bishop of Exeter gave his
clergy:

> My brethren I beg you will rise up with me against only moral
> preaching. We have been long attempting the reformation of
> the Nation by discourses of this kind. With what success? Why,
> none at all. On the contrary, we have very dexterously preached

the people into downright infidelity. We must change our voice; we must preach Christ and Him crucified. Nothing but the Gospel is, nothing will be found to be, the power of God unto salvation, besides. Let me, therefore, again and again request, may I add, *let me charge you*, to preach Jesus and salvation through his name; preach the Lord who brought the saying of the Great High Priest, 'He that believeth shall be saved.' Preach repentance towards God, and faith in our Lord Jesus Christ.[19]

This was a great encouragement to Charles whose hymns, like his preaching, had Jesus Christ at the centre. All this is brought to fruition in his 'conversion' hymn, 'Where Shall my Wondering Soul Begin?' John Wesley's 'conversion' experience described above was anticipated by brother Charles three days before on 21 May. Charles immediately wrote his conversion hymn and the two brothers sang it together on 24 May. The hymn begins with the bewilderment of the experience which he has had and moves on from there:

> Where shall my wondering soul begin?
> How shall I all to heaven aspire?
> A slave redeem'd from death and sin,
> A brand pluck'd from eternal fire,
> How shall I equal triumph raise,
> And sing my great Deliverer's praise?

Wesley sums up the position of all men and women who have turned to Christ in this verse. But he wants the appeal to go wider:

> Outcasts of men, to you I call,
> Harlots, and publicans, and thieves!
> He spreads His arms t'embrace you all;
> Sinners alone his grace receives;
> No need of Him the righteous have,
> He came the lost to seek and save.

When Charles was preaching to prisoners at Cardiff on 14 July 1741 this hymn was sung. Over twenty prisoners were thieves. His preaching obviously touched them and many tears were shed at the words 'Outcasts of men, to you I call'. The only way forward, both for the Wesleys and others, came in the last verse. The Wesleys began to grasp that one is justified before God by faith alone and not by anything we can do:

> For you the purple current flow'd
> In pardons from His wounded side;
> Languish'd for you th'eternal God,
> For you the Prince of Glory died.
> *Believe*, and all your guilt's forgiven.
> *Only believe* – and yours is heaven.[20]

Another common theme in Charles Wesley's hymns is the incarnation, though the atonement is never far away. Charles is the author of the well-known 'Hark! The Herald-angels Sing' (the original first line was 'Hark how all the welkin rings'). There were originally ten verses of four lines and among the omitted verses is:

> Now display Thy saving power,
> Ruin'd nature now restore;
> Now in mystic union join
> Thine to ours, and ours to Thine.

An emphasis on the incarnation in theology is one way of trying to make the Christian story relevant to its hearers. If the Wesleys could convince people that Jesus Christ was an ordinary human being, then there was some possibility that they would identify with him and they would therefore regard the faith as a real possibility. In the same way, an emphasis on the atonement shows that with a belief in Christ, people and circumstances can change and be redeemed, no matter how bad they may appear to be. But in order to want to be changed, people needed to be convinced that they were in a bad state in the first place. Hence in their 'pre-converted' state they were regarded as 'slaves', 'worms' and, in the hymn quoted above, as being ready for hell ('a brand plucked from eternal fire'). Virtually all of Wesley's hymns are based on Christ (as opposed to the Father or the Spirit) which means that salvation can only be found in Christ's fellowship, represented on earth by the Church or, in Wesley's view, by the Methodist Societies. Furthermore, salvation could only be assured within the fellowship

of Christ. Many members of the Methodist Societies would
have felt that they were of no consequence except through the
bounty and generosity of Christ which was a reflection of how
they would have regarded themselves in society at large, namely
that they were of no consequence except through the bounty
and generosity of their employers. In effect, the Methodist
Societies were a sacralization of the social status quo.

Like Watts, Wesley's hymns were personal, but unlike Watts
they were also individualistic. Thus the congregation would
conduct private devotions in audible unison instead of corporate praise with a common voice. People became children of
God and this identity was most keenly experienced within the
community of the believers – there was no attempt to allow
this to overflow into society at large. Indeed, the Wesleys wanted
to maintain the status quo as can be seen from this hymn from
the 1780 publication under the heading 'For Masters':

> Inferiors, as a sacred trust,
> I from the Sovereign Lord receive,
> That what is suitable and just,
> Impartial I to all may give:
>
> O'erlook them with a guardian eye;
> From vice and wickedness restrain;
> Mistakes and lesser faults pass by,
> And govern with a looser rein . . .
>
> Yet let me not my place forsake,
> The occasion of his stumbling prove,
> The servant to my bosom take,
> Or mar him by familiar love.[21]

The Wesleys made hymns truly popular, reflecting their style
of spreading the Gospel. They spent much of their time on the
road, preaching to the masses in the open air and deliberately
seeking out 'the fallen' in prisons and city streets. Through
preaching and hymns, the Wesleys provided people with a
much-needed approach to Christ which did not seem available
through the Established Church, but the hymns did contain

the Wesleys' social and political preferences, not only in the words but also in the way in which theology is used.

The hymns of the Wesleys were 'popular by destination', that is they were written by the Wesleys but were true expressions of the theology and spirituality of the people who sang them. We need to cross the Atlantic for examples of 'hymns' that were truly 'popular by origin', that is hymns that emerged from the community which sang them. These hymns, whose influence, power and genius have never been widely appreciated, are commonly known as Negro spirituals.

Negro Spirituals articulate the faith of an oppressed people and the hymns themselves are a means of liberation. It is difficult to comprehend the violence perpetrated against those who became slaves. They were torn away from their African homeland, tribes and customs. They had to travel across the sea cramped and manacled in the holds of ships, only being allowed out on occasion. Many died on the voyage: those who survived were forced to spend time in the darkness beside the corpses. When they reached their destination they faced the further indignity of being auctioned off. Any families that had survived intact were inevitably broken as husbands were separated from wives and children from their parents at the auction block. Out of this oppression came the Negro spirituals, which, according to James Cone, author of *The Spirituals and the Blues*, can only be understood by those who have experienced oppression:

> I am convinced it is not possible to render an authentic interpretation of black music without having shared and participated in the experience that created it. Black music must be *lived* before it can be understood.[22]

The Spirituals are very biblical, speaking of Moses, Joshua, Daniel, Jesus and the Holy Spirit. They are based on biblical stories, usually of liberation, which are applied directly to the slaves' situation. By singing these hymns, the power of God which liberated the heroes of the Bible is drawn upon in order to liberate the slaves:

> When Israel was in Egypt's land,
> Let my people go;

Oppressed so hard they could not stand,
Let my people go.

Refrain: Go down, Moses, 'way down in Egypt's land;
Tell ole Pharaoh
Let my people go.

'Thus saith the Lord,' bold Moses said,
Let my people go;
If not I'll smite your first-born dead,
Let my people go.

No more shall they in bondage toil,
Let my people go;
Let them come out with Egypt's spoil,
Let my people go.

The Lord told Moses what to do,
Let my people go;
To lead the children of Israel thro'
Let my people go.

When they had reached the other shore,
Let my people go;
They sang a song of triumph 'oer,
Let my people go.

And:

My Lord delivered Daniel,
My Lord delivered Daniel,
My Lord delivered Daniel,
Why can't He deliver me?

The existence of the Negro Spirituals is a testimony to how a people forged a theology of offence and defence out of a psychological shackle. When the slave was cut off from his people, he was also cut off from his religion, whatever kind it was. Christianity was the religion of the slave-master: indeed, it frequently justified the inhuman action of the slave-master, but by some incredible spiritual insight the slaves took on the religion that the master had profaned in their midst, made it their own and transformed it from being a justification of slavery to becoming a means of liberation. Let us consider two examples of this.

In Jeremiah 8, the prophet comes to a great depression in his life. He is distressed over the external events of Israel and he is also spiritually depressed and tortured when he cries out in verse 22:

> Is there not balm in Gilead any more?
> Is there no doctor there?

Jeremiah utters this cry in the midst of his soul-searching when, stripped bare of everything, he is brought face to face with the core of his own faith. He is in fact saying that surely there must be balm in Gilead. The slaves caught the mood of this dilemma because they had actually shared such an ordeal and the result is a hymn that actually answers Jeremiah's deep questioning from their own experience:

> There is a balm in Gilead,
> To make the spirit whole.
> There is a balm in Gilead,
> To heal the sin-sick soul.

The second example is well illustrated from the hymn:

> I got shoes, you got shoes,
> All God's children got shoes.
> When we get to Heaven
> We're goin' to put on our shoes
> An' shout all over God's Heaven.
> Heaven! Heaven!
> But everybody talking 'bout Heaven
> Ain't going there.

Slaves would have heard talk of heaven, the final abode of the righteous, from his master. Naturally the master reckoned himself as fitting that category. Yet the slave knew that he too would be going to heaven. He then thought that there must be two separate heavens, but then realized that the righteousness

and justice of God would not allow such a thing. The slave
continued to reason that he was having his hell now and that
when he dies, he will be having his heaven. Conversely, the
master was having his heaven now and when he dies he will be
having his hell. So when the slaves sang about shoes (which
they would not have on earth but which were symbols of true
wealth) they believed that they already had them waiting for
them in heaven. However, the last two lines of the verse referred
to their masters whom they believed would not go to heaven.

These were real songs of revolt. Any masters hearing them
would probably not have understood their significance, perhaps
wondering why their slaves were singing of Moses and Daniel
– maybe even pleased that their slaves had accepted the Christian faith. Like the book of Daniel to the oppressed Jews, the
Negro Spirituals were hymns of liberation, sung in a code which
only those who shared oppression could understand. But the
most revolutionary element of the spirituals were the parts that
at first glance appear to be escapist. The spirituals frequently
refer to heaven and the slaves look forward to going there:

> Good Lord, shall I ever be de one
> To get over in de Promise' Lan'?

And

> I want to be ready
> To walk in Jerusalem just like John.

And

> Swing low, sweet chariot,
> Comin' for to carry me home.

The constant references to heaven are enduring reminders
to the slaves that they are already liberated. They know that
they are God's children, that God is just and righteous and
that God loves them and will not let them down. In God's eyes
they are human beings made in God's image: nothing that the
slave-masters can say or do can remove this truth, reality and
dignity. The future is a reality that has already happened in
Jesus' resurrection: they are already free, it is just a matter of
time before it becomes a reality. The slaves' existence tran-

scended historical limitations. The Spiritual which reveals that they knew that slavery was not their real destiny and that it would not last for ever was:

> Oh Freedom! Oh Freedom!
> Oh, Freedom, I love thee!
> And before I'll be a slave,
> I'll be buried in my grave,
> And go home to my Lord and be free.

For the slaves and still for many people today, singing did not simply point to the Gospel but it was the medium through which liberation was worked out.

One of the major differences between the theology of the hymns of Wesley and the Negro Spirituals is that freedom for members of the Methodist Societies came by acknowledgement of their sinfulness and of God's grace, mediated through Jesus Christ, which could only be received by withdrawing from the world to the fellowship of Christ's people; however, the spirituals acknowledge the slaves as children of God who need saving, not from themselves, but from the slavery imposed by the world. The hymns of Wesley enable the singers to experience freedom within the Societies: the Spirituals enable the singers to experience freedom in the world.

4

From 'Amazing Grace!' to 'O Valiant Hearts'

Music is to the soul what wind is to the ship, blowing her onwards in the direction in which she is steered . . . Not allowed to sing that tune or this tune? Indeed! Secular music, do you say? Belongs to the devil, does it? Well, if it did, I would plunder him of it . . . Every note and every strain and every harmony is divine and belongs to us.

William Booth

Negro Spirituals were not the only creative outcome of the inhumanity of the slave trade: hymn-writer John Newton was another. Born in 1725, Newton was a talented and frequently troubled person. His mother (who died just before his seventh birthday) was a practising religious Dissenter and his father was a ship's master. Newton's mother was a powerful influence in his upbringing, introducing him early to prayer and Scripture. Newton was, unwillingly, a naval man where, in his earlier years, he had a chequered career: being press-ganged into the service, he deserted, was recaptured, put in irons and flogged with the cat o'nine tails. However, Newton, of his own free will, continued at sea where he began work in the service of the slave trade.

Newton was a heavy drinker and enjoyed twisting and distorting words of Scripture which he had learnt under the influence of his mother – many who heard Newton felt that he was risking the wrath of God through his churlish language and behaviour. It was on a trip from Cape Lopez to England that disaster struck *The Greyhound* on which Newton was sailing. A huge wave nearly overwhelmed the ship and in order to survive Newton lashed himself to the wheel and steered the ship for

eleven hours. Then he turned to the God whom he had blas-
phemed and began to pray. Eventually the storm abated and
Newton arrived home safely. This incident is behind what must
be Newton's most famous hymn – references to his hazardous
sea-trip are clear in both verses:

> Amazing grace! (how sweet the sound)
> That sav'd a wretch like me!
> I once was lost, but now am found,
> Was blind, but now I see . . .
>
> Thro' many dangers, toils and snares,
> I have already come;
> 'Tis grace has brought me safe thus far,
> And grace will lead me home.

After this incident, Newton felt a calling by God to the
ordained ministry, yet continued in the slave trade, seeing no
conflict between this and his calling. The Church of England
was initially suspicious of Newton with his naval and Dissenting
background, but eventually he was ordained and became curate
at Olney (which lies between Northampton and Bedford). In
his curacy, Newton became a close friend to William Cowper,
the lay curate, and together they wrote the *Olney Hymns* which
was published in 1799. This collection was compiled with the
object of:

> promoting the faith and comfort of sincere Christians . . . and
> as a monument to perpetuate the remembrance of an intimate
> and endeared friendship.[1]

The story of Newton illustrates two important points. First,
how the incidents within a person's life are the stuff out of
which hymns are written: grace is a common theme in Newton's
hymns which tend to have in the background how God saved
the reprobate from death at sea and constantly saves him
from the death of sin. Secondly, it was such collections as the
Olney Hymns which were to force the hand of the Church of
England to accept hymns within its worship. The Church was
suspicious of hymns because they were associated with the
'Dissent' of the Nonconformists, the 'enthusiasm' of the

Methodists and the 'personal experience' of the Evangelicals. Hitherto, various private collections were being used, but the Church establishment refused to acknowledge them, arguing that the psalmody of the 'Old' and 'New Versions' were the only songs permissible in Church. However, pressure was growing: psalm-singing was deteriorating badly and many congregations were agitating for hymns. Indeed, even the 'Old' and 'New Versions' were printed with supplements of hymns. Newton and Cowper with the *Olney Hymns* were examples of Evangelicals accepting hymns as an important part of their spirituality, thereby putting pressure on the Church as a whole to do the same.

The collection was divided into three books, the first containing 141 hymns 'On Selected Texts of Scripture', the second 100 hymns 'On Occasional Subjects' and the third 107 hymns 'On the Rise, Progress, Changes and Comforts of the Spiritual Life'. The hymns in the collection include: 'Glorious Things of Thee are Spoken', 'How Sweet the Name of Jesus Sounds', 'Great Shepherd of thy People, Hear', 'May the Grace of Christ our Saviour' as well as 'Amazing Grace!' (all by Newton); 'Sometimes a Light Surprises the Christian while he Sings', 'Jesus, Where'er thy People Meet', 'O for a Closer Walk with God', 'Hark, my Soul, it is the Lord' (all by Cowper). What is significant about this particular collection is that it showed that substantial hymn-writers could come out of the Church of England as well as the Nonconformist Churches. However, the authors are vague as to the actual aims of the hymns and how they fit within the liturgy of the Church of England. Later collections will determine their function within Anglican worship just as the Wesleys did for Methodist worship.

Another unexpected area through which hymns found their way into the Established Church was the charity schools and institutions. At such institutions as the Foundling Hospital (founded 1738), the Lock Hospital (1756) and the Asylum or House of Refuge for Female Orphans (1758) the inmates had special hymn books published for them, so there appeared *Psalms and Hymns for the Chapel of the Asylum or House of Refuge for Female Orphans*, first published in the 1760s and *Psalms, Hymns and Anthems of the Foundling Hospital*, published in 1774.

Singing became a recognized feature within these institutions. In addition, the charity children led the singing in a number of parish churches, taking the place of a choir. As well as improving the quality of psalm-singing, the children brought hymns into churches. Fundraising services led by the massed voices of children from these institutions became common and welcome features of eighteenth-century Church life. The first united service of this kind was held at St Andrew's, Holborn, in 1704. From 1782 until 1877 these gatherings were held in St Paul's Cathedral.

Some hymns written for the children of these institutions are still sung today: for example, 'Praise the Lord! Ye Heav'ns Adore Him' (from the *Foundling Hospital Collection* – based on Psalm 148), 'Spirit of Mercy, Truth and Love' (*Foundling Hospital Collection*) and 'Lead us, Heav'nly Father, Lead us' (a hymn written for the London Orphan Asylum). Indeed, knowing the place for which the latter hymn was written enables us to understand how the children and their environment were viewed. The world is clearly a 'tempestuous' place and so they need God's (and their guardians') protection – 'guard us, guide us, keep us, feed us'. They also admit to their 'weakness':

> Lead us, heavenly Father, lead us
> o'er the world's tempestuous sea;
> guard us, guide us, keep us, feed us,
> for we have no help but thee;
> yet possessing every blessing,
> if our God our Father be.
>
> Saviour, breathe forgiveness o'er us:
> all our weakness thou dost know;
> thou didst tread this earth before us,
> thou didst feel its keenest woe . . .

A number of the hymns from these institutions affirm and encourage the generosity of the benefactors to the institutions:

> Each Hand and Heart that lent us Aid,
> Thou didst inspire and guide;

> Nor shall their Love be unrepaid,
> Who for the Poor provide.

And clearly indicate the place of the children:

> Thy gracious hand, to diff'rent ranks
> Hath diff'rent lots assign'd;
> 'Tis ours to tread the lower path,
> And bear a humble mind.[2]

Another indication of the popular appeal of hymns can be seen in the funeral hymn. There is evidence that England once possessed a tradition of songs depicting the journey of the soul to the next world. Evidence suggests that these songs were an amalgam of Catholicism and popular belief. Manuscripts of village Church musicians and printed sources provide a good idea of funeral hymns in use between the middle of the eighteenth and nineteenth centuries. In contrast to the earlier hymns these were thoroughly Protestant in their theology, neglecting the journey of the soul but using death as an opportunity for calling the living to repentance and invoking the scene of the Last Judgement. The burial service in the Book of Common Prayer did not provide a place for such hymns but they were sung during the procession to the church, maybe (with a tolerant minister) during the service, but certainly after it. This custom of the funeral hymn was very powerful because it enabled the mourners to feel that they had an active part of sending the deceased on his or her journey. The power of the custom can be seen by the fact that although in the middle of the nineteenth century clergy refused permission for the funeral hymn to be sung, mourners, nevertheless, returned to the grave after the clergyman had departed in order to pay their respects in the traditional way.

The pressure for the Church of England to accept formally what had been happening informally was becoming irresistible. While some parishes compiled their own collections of hymns, some bishops banned their use from their dioceses. Among the objections about hymns were that they introduced false doctrines or undermined Church doctrines and they offended against the reverence of worship by the flippancy and vulgarity of some of the words and tunes. There were some within the Church who were concerned that the power and control which they had over their congregations were being threatened by the voice that the populace was acquiring in theology and worship through the hymns that they enjoyed. The matter came to a head in 1819. Thomas Cotterill, vicar of St Paul's Church, Sheffield, tried to enforce the use of his hymnal entitled *A Selection of Psalms and Hymns for Public and Private Use, Adapted to the Services of the Church of England* on his congregation. Some of the congregation reacted against Cotterill's book and there was a disturbance within his church. Outside, opponents of hymns also took advantage of the dispute. There was a legal suit against Cotterill which was heard in the Church's Consistery Court under the jurisdiction of the Archbishop of York. The Chancellor (the chief Church law officer in the diocese) admitted that hymn-singing was a popular practice that could be an aid to faith and devotion and yet there was no provision within the Book of Common Prayer for its use. Consequently he ruled that hymn-singing was an irregularity without due authority, but it was felt that none could attack a practice that had become so widespread and was clearly so edifying. He refused costs and postponed sentence upon Cotterill. The Archbishop mediated in the case, Cotterill's book was withdrawn and a new book (*A Selection of Psalms and Hymns for Public Worship*), which was smaller and less evangelical, was prepared under the eye of the Archbishop and at his expense.

Although there were still some opponents of hymn-singing, no further legal actions ensued. Thus it was not until the second decade of the nineteenth century that hymn-singing was officially recognized in the Church of England: it was only after this time that it became widely accepted within the Church of England.

Officially allowing hymns within the Church of England was one matter, but what purpose would they serve? The Methodists used their hymns to construct their service; indeed, one could say that for Methodists the hymns *were* their service. But for Anglicans the Book of Common Prayer fulfilled this function. It was a vicar in the Shropshire parish of Hodnet, Reginald Heber, who provided an answer in his hymn book *Hymns*

Written and Adapted to the Weekly Church Service of the Year.
The book was published in 1827 (one year after the death of
Heber, who had become Bishop of Calcutta) though it had
been prepared some years earlier. Heber designed his book for
public worship and arranged hymns not only for Sunday
worship and to accompany the sacraments, but also for the
great festivals of the Church, for 'national occasions of thanksgiving or distress', for 'after the sermon', 'for morning', 'for
evening' and 'for funerals'. Heber thereby provided hymns to
accompany the liturgy of the Church. There were two other
significant features in Heber's book. First, he put the psalm-
version of hymns within their appropriate sections rather than
giving them a position of privilege on their own. Secondly, he
included some of the old Latin hymns drawn from a seven-
teenth-century Office Book reflecting the concern of a certain
section of the Church, that was to reach its climax in the
Oxford Movement, to return to the wisdom and influence of the
Church's more Catholic roots. A number of the hymns in
Heber's book are frequently sung today: 'Holy, Holy, Holy!
Lord God Almighty', 'From Greeland's Icy Mountains', 'The
Son of God Goes Forth to War', 'Ride on! Ride on in Majesty'.

It was John Keble with his hymn book *The Christian Year*
(which opens with the hymns 'New Every Morning is the Love'
and 'Sun of my Soul! Thou Saviour Dear') who was concerned
to draw English hymn-writing into the Catholic tradition of the
Oxford Movement and to raise the literary standard of hymns.
Like Heber, he drew on some old Latin hymns of the Catholic
Church in order to reclaim some of the spirituality and tradition
of the Church which had been cast aside at the Reformation.
The Christian Year (published in 1827) arranges hymns for the
liturgical year and for such occasions as the Burial of the Dead,
the Churching of Women and even for the Gunpowder Trea-
son. Hitherto, popular hymnody had been dominated by Evangelicals, whose hymns had become the voice of the individual
believer; the hymns drawn from the offices of the Catholic
Church became the voice of the worshipping Church.

The hymn, which is a popular response to and expression of
faith, was now becoming more literary and more liturgical. It
was the appeal of its more literary aspects that made it

acceptable in English public schools which published their own hymn books. The earliest service books were those for Rugby in 1824 and Leeds Grammar School in 1826. Rugby's had only four hymns. In the 1843 edition it had fifty-six hymns and eighteen psalms and by 1897 it had around 360 hymns in elaborate liturgical sequence. Public school hymn books are very good examples of how hymns reflect and shape the position and aspirations of those who sing them: they have also had a significant effect on the Christian faith in this country. Lionel Adey, formerly Professor of English at the University of Victoria in Canada, has done a great deal of work on this theme and I am indebted to Adey for the fruits of his research used here.

Let us now consider in some detail a publication which is seminal in the story of modern hymnody: *Hymns Ancient and Modern*. S. T. Bindoff in his book *Tudor England* wrote:

> Cranmer could not render the hymns of the Catholic Breviary into singable English and three centuries were to pass before 'Hymns Ancient and Modern' was to complete, with the Book of Common Prayer and the Authorized Version, the splendid trilogy with which the Anglican Church has endowed the English-speaking world.[3]

Just as Watts and the Wesleys were important figures in the development of the hymn, so too was the publication of *Hymns Ancient and Modern*. From the publication of this book in 1861 it is hymn books rather than hymn-writers which have most influence on the hymn, since the way that a hymn is received depends a great deal on the section of the hymn book in which it is located. The power of the hymn book editor surpasses that of the hymn-writer.

The evolution of *Hymns Ancient and Modern* can best be understood in its historical context. In the middle of the nineteenth century Evangelicals, who had been using hymns for a long time, were content with their various collections of hymn books, but, in the wake of the Oxford Movement, those who regarded themselves as High Church wanted to cultivate the musical side of their liturgies. A committee was formed under the dynamic leadership of Sir Henry W. Baker, vicar of Monkland, Hertfordshire, to compile a book which would express the devotion and spirituality of those in sympathy with the Oxford Movement. Baker himself insisted that as well as taking hymns from more traditional sources it was important:

> to give among the general hymns some that would be suitable for singing in mission rooms, at lectures in cottages, etc., rather than in church. We want such and this would give 'good grounds' on which to admit some as to which we should otherwise feel bound to be more strict.[4]

A specimen booklet of fifty hymns was circulated in May 1859 and many hundreds of clergy and laity had the opportunity of commenting. The name 'Ancient and Modern' exactly expresses the purpose of the book. Its primary purpose was to restore to the devotion of the Church of England the treasures of Latin hymnody (the compilers seem to have treated the seventeenth- and eighteenth-century hymns of Paris – taken from the 'Paris Breviary' – as ancient), but it was also considered important to include a considerable number of modern hymns in order to ensure a favourable reception. The book was a huge success. The extent of the success can be seen from the report of a Convocation Committee of the Convocation of Canterbury set up in 1871 to consider the desirability of a uniform hymn book for the Church of England. *Hymns Ancient and Modern* was the prime candidate. In 1892 the Committee gave provisional figures about the circulation of hymnals and it was discovered that in England 10,237 Anglican churches used *Hymns Ancient and Modern*, 1,420 used *Hymnal Companion* and 372 used other hymn books. *Hymns Ancient and Modern*, still a popular book under its revised title *Hymns Ancient and Modern New Standard*, has gone through a number of revisions and has had various supplements.

In his book *Religion and Society in Industrial England*, historian A. D. Gilbert convincingly argues that the Anglican Church allied itself with the establishment in order that it should not lose its privileges, and in a similar way extra-establishment Protestantism allied itself with the up-and-coming industrial classes. The Church of England had its heart in the rural areas and, with the English governing classes, held a low view of commerce and industry, considering the city 'vulgar' or 'for the

vulgar'. *Hymns Ancient and Modern*, with all its comprehensive-
ness and liberality, is very much a product of the Established
Church. There is a strong link with agricultural imagery in the
hymns in a society where the urban areas were gaining importance in the nation's life (the nation's wealth was becoming more
dependent upon the factories in the towns). This indicates a
social nostalgia as well as an indication that the writers and
compilers of these hymns, alongside the heart of the Church
of England, are firmly placed in the countryside.

The theology of the book provides a legitimization of the
status quo. Like the rulers of the land, God the Father is
frequently remote from this world, dwelling far above it, in the
height of heaven:

> God from on high . . . (58 v. 1)[5]

> O My God, I fear Thee
> Thou art very high (567 v. 1)

When there is an emphasis on a remote God, there is no strong
requirement of loyalty to the Church since power and authority
are so far away as to have little meaning or influence. This
pattern of authority is reflected in society. God is frequently
addressed as 'Lord' and 'King'. This understanding of power
and powerfulness reflected the establishment (with its lords and
Queen), thereby providing a divine imprimatur on the status
quo. There is also a stress on submissiveness and social conservatism which provides a model of how one relates to power
and authority:

> And give their flocks a lowly mind
> To hear and to obey (354 v. 6).

Paradise in an after-life is promised as compensation for the
sufferings of this world which encourages people to endure
their current lot and not shake the establishment:

> Where no pain nor sorrow,
> Toil nor care is known (305 v. 3).

Even though some hymns explicitly condemn money and
material wealth –

> Jesus calls us from the worship
> Of the vain world's golden store (403 v. 3)

– heaven is, nevertheless, described in terms of conspicuous wealth, thereby giving sanction to the pursuit and acquisition of wealth:

> When shall these eyes thy heaven-built walls
> And pearly gates behold?
> Thy bulwarks with salvation strong,
> And streets of shining gold? (236 v. 2)

The relationship between God and the poor is one of condescension which reflected contemporary relationships between rich and poor, powerful and powerless:

> The Son of God his glory hides
> With parents mean and poor . . .
>
> The Maker of the stars on high
> An humble trade pursues (78 vv. 2, 3).

Hymns Ancient and Modern also legitimizes the establishment's imperialist expansion policies by the military imagery used in the missionary hymns:

> Ye armies of the living God
> Sworn warriors of Christ's host . . .
> Strong in your captain's mighty strength
> Go to the conquest of all lands (586 v. 4).
>
> For all the wreaths of Empire
> Meet upon His brow (306 v. 7).

Military conquest is also affirmed in service of God and nation as in 'O Lord, be with us When we Sail':

> If duty calls from threaten'd strife
> To guard our native shore,
> And shot and shell are answering fast
> The booming cannon's roar,

Be Thou the mainguard of our host,
Till war and danger cease:
Defend the right, put up the sword,
And through the world make peace (592 vv. 4, 5)

Not all hymn books endorsed the status quo. In 1838 *Hymns for Anti-Slavery Prayer Meetings* was published in London. According to the Preface, profits from its sale were to go to the 'Sheffield Ladies' Association for the Universal Abolition of Slavery.'[6] There are only nine hymns in this collection, but it is a reminder of how hymns support the social and theological position of the writers. What is also of great interest is that these hymns come from the pens of writers who are contributors to the more established hymn books. Hymns were written expressly for this collection by Josiah Conder (well known for 'Bread of Heaven, on Thee we Feed' and 'The Lord is King! Lift up thy Voice'), by James Montgomery (well known for 'Angels, from the Realms of Glory' and 'Stand Up and Bless the Lord'), as well as by contemporary hymn-writers Bernard Barton and Ann Gilbert. The hymns are uncompromising in their attack on the institution of slavery:

Liberty-imparting Spirit!
Breathe on Afric's fettered race;
That, through thee, they may inherit
This divinest gift of grace.

Thou canst break their bonds asunder,
Thou canst cast their yoke away;
Speak! and in a voice of thunder,
Which the oppressor must obey.

Tell the man who dares to barter
In his brother's flesh and blood,
He has broken the high charter
Of our common brotherhood!

And for this will stand indicted
At the judgement-seat on high,

There to be by God required
For usurped authority!

But to the oppressed, heart-broken,
Speak in tones of gentlest love;
And may every word, thus spoken,
Bear a blessing from above.

Tell them of a freedom greater
Than of man was ever won;
Given them by their Creator,
In his Spirit, through his Son!

Where that Spirit has possession
Of his heart, the slave is free;
And in spite of man's oppression,
Is a child of liberty.

This hymn is reminiscent of the twentieth-century 'social gospel' hymns of Fred Kaan and Brian Wren. Although the Creator God is far away, the caring nature of God is expressed through the Spirit. Another hymn is written especially for women and contrasts how the sin of the 'fathers' can be undone by the 'mothers':

We can but weep, while Thou canst aid,
We can but pray, – Thou, Lord, canst save!
Deliverance, e'en as thou hast said,
We for our father's victims crave.

The widow's mite, the orphan's prayer,
The tear of pitying poverty,
Our hands, our voices, shall declare
A nation's deep repentant cry . . .

Mothers in Israel – daughters – wives,
On Britain's as on Judah's shore,
To freedom's cause devote your lives,
Servants of God, serve sin no more!

Montgomery, perhaps more than the other writers, is able to set the cause for which the book was compiled with a dignity and in a context against which many arguments would appear puny:

> The gates of brass our Saviour broke,
> The bars of iron he overthrew,
> To lighten every galling yoke,
> And every manacle undo;
> From man, man's bondsman to set free,
> Captive he led captivity.
>
> Lord, as from sin, death, hell, thy power
> Unchains the souls to thee that cry,
> Of slavery bid the final hour,
> Of Jubilee the first, draw nigh;
> Oh! haste to set the Negro free,
> And captive lead captivity.

Such hymns did not find their way into the major collections, but they do reveal how hymns can assist in articulating sentiments which were at the time quite radical. These hymns also reveal how hymns can unashamedly be employed as a means to support political ends.

We have already seen how the hymns sung by children at the charity schools reflected their school position; so too did the hymns sung in the public schools. Jonathan Gathorne-Hardy in *The Public-School Phenomenon* wrote:

> But public schools had their own corpus of . . . songs that echo down the nineteenth century and deep into the twentieth . . . the splendid hymns of the Church of England, collected together in 'Hymns Ancient and Modern.' Hymns bound the public schools together.[7]

A study of the hymns sung in the English public schools reveals a whole range of churchmanships. Wellington College published a hymn book in 1880 that resembled a breviary; Clifton in 1885 published a collection representing a central Anglican tradition; Uppingham and Sherborne (1874) published hymnals set in a more Broad Church tradition with a stress on 'muscular Christianity' – hymns of praise and pilgrimage oust sentimentality. Towards the end of the century, a number of the public schools shared many hymns and the great majority of them from *Hymns Ancient and Modern*.[8] This would not be surprising since the pupils at these schools would have been the sons and daughters of those who attended the churches at which *Hymns Ancient and Modern* (with all its theological emphases) would have been sung. What was surprising was that the hymns from *Hymns Ancient and Modern* which they did sing, although confirming their social status, were not as military and aggressive as many of their contemporaries and seniors would have been singing outside their schools. 'Forth in thy Name, O Lord, I go, my Daily Labour to Pursue', 'We Plough the Fields and Scatter the Good Seed on the Land', 'Thine Arm, O Lord, in Days of Old, was Strong to Heal and Save', all encourage the singers to service and to improve the lot of the unfortunate. Also they would have sung 'Here, O my Lord, I see Thee Face to Face' and 'I Heard the Voice of Jesus Say': in their self-contained communities, these young people were not singing hymns that reflected a faith distorted by jingo-ism and sentimentality, but they tended to sing about service. It was this generation that supplied administrators and senior officers who played a key role in the First World War.

One group of people which remained, by and large, untouched by the Church was the working class. The Church was an essentially middle-class institution with middle-class values in which members of the working class felt alienated. At the time of the Prince of Wales' illness in 1871, the Archbishop of Canterbury caused prayers to be said for his recovery: but the Archbishop did not cause prayers to be said at a mining disaster – and people noticed this. Evangelists of the working classes wanted them to change their ways, but did not want anybody to change the social conditions in which they lived. There were occasions when families, having no choice but to work on Sundays, were warned against working on the Sabbath. To say that the working classes had been untouched by the Church is not to say that they had no religious beliefs, but it is to say that the Churches (Established and Noncon-formist) did not articulate faith in a way that accommodated working-class values. The Churches neither represented them in their institutions nor did they offer any way out of their poverty. However, the working classes did sing hymns. We have already heard about the funeral hymn; so too a feature of their Whit walks (over the Whit weekend was a break from work when these walks were undertaken) was the singing of hymns.

The nearest we get to hymns for the working classes is in the Gospel hymns of Moody and Sankey. Dwight L. Moody and Ira D. Sankey adopted the patterns of Evangelism from their native North America and concentrated on evangelizing the huge populations of the urban areas at meetings which took place in tents and halls as much as in churches. Moody was the preacher and Sankey was the soloist who moved so many with his singing. In terms of Evangelism, Moody and Sankey had limited success, mainly with people who were on the edges of Church life and needed encouragement to become more committed: their appeal was mainly to people from the middle and lower-middle class. But their hymns were very popular with their memorable tunes and simple, direct and sentimental lyrics. In most of the hymns the verse was sung by a soloist and everybody joined in the chorus. They wanted to appeal to the emotions and they did this very effectively, thereby offering a similar entry into believing and faith to that provided over a century earlier by the Wesleys. Their hymns (published in *Sacred Hymns and Solos*) are still popular today in Revivalist circles and their sales in Britain, which reached eighty million by the 1950s, have equalled those of *Hymns Ancient and Modern*.

In his preaching (and Sankey reflected this in the hymns) Moody secularized heaven and hell. He identified heaven with the culture of his hearers, a kind of middle-class home, with labour ended, the table spread, goodness all round, lost ones restored and hymnody incessant. For many, the harsh realities of industrial cities did not provide any hope in this world, and so they were encouraged not to engage with their environment, but to look elsewhere for respite. There was a nostalgia for the countryside which would have appealed to the city dwellers:

When the mists have rolled in splendour
From the beauty of the hills.
And the sunlight falls in gladness,
On the river and the rills,
We recall our Father's promise
In the rainbow of the spray:
We shall know each other better
When the mists have rolled away.

Chorus: We shall know as we are known,
Never more to walk alone. . . .

Heaven is identified with home: 'Sins and Sorrows, Strifes and Fears' hints at how this world is viewed:

Beyond the light of setting suns,
Beyond the clouded sky,
Beyond where starlight fades in night
I have a home on high.

Chorus: A mansion there not made with hands,
A place prepared for me;
And while God lives, and angels sing
That home my home shall be.

My sins and sorrows, strifes and fears,
I bid them all farewell,
High up amid th'eternal years,
With Christ, my Lord, to dwell . . .

In the following hymn heaven is seen as a place of family reunion:

Over the river faces I see,
Fair as the morning, looking for me;
Free from their sorrow, grief and despair,
Waiting and watching patiently there.

Chorus: Looking this way, yes, looking this way,
Loved ones are waiting looking this way;

> Fair as the morning, bright as the day,
> Dear ones in glory looking this way.
>
> Father and mother safe in the vale . . .
>
> Brother and sister gone to that clime,
> Wait for the others coming some time . . . [9]

These hymns had moved far from Scripture and attempted to open the channel of faith through feeling and sentiment. The Wesleys acknowledged the importance of emotion in their hymns but the subject was always unashamedly Christ crucified. The hymns of Ira Sankey were, in essence, far more secular and do not engage in the theological struggle between text (the biblical message) and context (the world to which the hymns were directed).

Just as the family and the life to come were made sacred in the hymns of the lower classes, so the nation, Church and Empire, which was fast expanding, were made sacred in the hymns of the upper classes. God was still transcendent, but also immanent in the institutions which were regarded as sacred:

> O let no foe draw nigh
> Nor lawless deed of crime
> Insult Thy Majesty.
> O Lord, stretch forth Thy mighty hand,
> And guard and bless our Fatherland (142 v. 8).

In 'For Thy Dear Saint, O Lord':

> Thine earthly members fit
> To join Thy Saints above,
> In one communion ever knit,
> One fellowship of love (448 v. 3).

And in 'To Thee and to thy Christ, O God':

> To Thee and to thy Christ, O God,
> We sing – we ever sing;
> For he hath crushed beneath His rod
> The world's proud rebel king,

> He plunged in His imperial strength
> The gulfs of darkness down (502 v. 3).

These last three hymns come from *Hymns Ancient and Modern*, the upper-middle-class book of the establishment.

Victorian hymns did not consecrate industrial work and the environment of the cities, but they were nostalgic for the countryside which they portrayed in romantic terms. The details of the sacred story were being pushed to the edge of hymns and were being used as means of entry into the hymn-writer's reflections on contemporary society. These reflections were expressed in imagery which revealed the writer's interests and concerns. The hymn in which this secularization reaches its climax is J. S. Arkwright's 'O Valiant Hearts, who to your Glory Came' which was published in 1919. The first part of the hymn tells of the honour in which those who sacrifice their lives for their country will be held. Highly charged words like 'valiant' and 'knightly' encourage patriotism:

> O valiant hearts, who to your glory came
> Through dust of conflict and through battle flame;
> Tranquil you lie, your knightly virtue proved,
> Your memory hallowed in the name you loved.

The second part of the hymn compares the sacrifice of those who have fallen in battle with the great sacrifice at Calvary. Those who have died for their country will rise in the same way that Christ rose from the dead. Love of country and love of God are the same. The secularization of the faith is reflected in the secularization in the hymn:

> These were his servants, in his steps they trod,
> Following through death the martyred Son of God:
> Victor he rose; victorious too shall rise
> They who have drunk his cup of sacrifice.

Hymn-writers were now using the symbols of faith to make sense of the world: this contrasted with the psalmists who used the world to make sense of their faith. Hymns were now beginning to treat as an end what had previously been regarded as a means. It was becoming clear that the secularization which was happening in society was being reflected in hymns.

5

The Hymn Explosion

A good hymn is the most difficult thing in the world to write. The wonder is that we have so many of them.

Alfred Lord Tennyson

There have been periods of frenetic hymn activity in the past: over 450 different metrical psalters and 250 hymn books were published in the eighteenth century; in the Church of England alone between 1830 and 1880 an average of one hymn book a year was produced. But over the last thirty-five years there has been a real explosion of hymns in these islands. The word 'explosion' is so appropriate because hymns have been appearing from all kinds of directions, with some making more of an impact than others and some being more illuminating than others.[1] These hymns have been a theological response and challenge to the great changes occurring in society as a whole and they have played no small part in enabling and encouraging the Church to interact with these changes. One of the things that is very difficult to chart is the dynamic of the interaction. There can be no doubt that the Christian faith was affected by changes in the world around: but how much influence did the Christian faith have on the way that society reacted to these changes?

Hymns make sense of the changes in society within the framework of faith. Furthermore, hymns reveal how various parts of the Church react in accordance with their own theological preferences; thus some hymns encourage withdrawal from the world, others fuller engagement. As a result of this, early in these explosive years different divisions within the Church were apparent from the hymns that were sung, so the charismatics had their hymns, the Evangelicals had theirs, Catholics had theirs and those advocating a more social Gospel had theirs. However, in this last decade of the century an ecumenical spirit has encouraged a willingness for these groups to discuss and learn from each other in consequence of which their worship and theology have been enriched.

When great changes (be they in the field of personal relationships or in the way that a society is ordered) do occur, they may be sudden, but they are rarely unexpected. The issues which force such changes will have been around for some time, but changes will only occur successfully when the time is right: the real skill is knowing when that time has come and managing the change creatively. In this chapter we shall be considering the changes in the fabric of society, some theological responses to them and how hymns reflect upon these changes. We shall concentrate on the events of the 1960s and 1970s since these were particularly volatile times from which we are still learning. Remembering that hymns are Christian folk-songs, it is possible to see how the thoughts and feelings of those people in the pew, whose theology is reflected in the hymns, have entered and perhaps even shaped the theological debate. Among the great technological revolutions over the last thirty-five years are the photocopier and micro-chip. The result of such technology is that the physical reproduction of hymns is so much easier and, combined with the over-head projector, has meant that more hymns are readily accessible to more people. Contemporary access to this technology reminds us how remarkable was the achievement in hymn production of our eighteenth- and ninteenth-century forebears.

The 1950s saw a period of post-war consenses and comparative stability which was summed up in Harold Macmillan's comment to the country that they had 'never had it so good'. Macmillan's remark epitomized an underlying belief that material wealth was the mark of success and the gateway to power. By contrast, the 1960s were years of great upheaval and uncertainty when dearly held assumptions and understandings were subjected to acute questioning, criticism and self-examination. The issues of these years are still on the agenda today. The British Empire, which was a symbol of power and pride in the 1950s, was becoming smaller as many countries in the developing world were edging towards independence. The unity of the nation which the Second World War and the post-war years had secured was being threatened as people asked penetrating questions about wealth, poverty and authority. Technology was moving at an unsettling rate. The 1960s were on the threshold of commercializing the micro-chip, it was now possible to launch a man into space, there was progress in medical science which resulted in people living longer. The question going through many minds was whether there was any limit to human achievement: we can go into space, can we conquer it? We can do a great deal in medical science, can we enable people to live for ever? At the same time, there were more disturbing advances. With new and exciting technology came the unleashing of nuclear power whose lethal potential had been demonstrated with the dropping of the atom bomb on Hiroshima. For the first time, people became aware that the destruction of the whole planet was a possibility and the growing tension between East and West brought this closer. The Cuban Missile Crisis in 1962 made the world aware of the fragility of its future. Today the threat of nuclear annihilation may have receded (although the rise of nationalism in countries of the former Soviet Union keep this issue alive), but it has been replaced with the possibility of ecological disaster.

Another shift taking place at this time was that in political power blocs. Great Britain was no longer the world power it had been and countries belonging to what had been called the third world were taking more power and authority to themselves. The oil crisis of 1973 during which the oil-producing Arab nations virtually held the West to ransom, was a strong lesson about the necessity for a different political understanding – since this discovery of their economic potential, a number of Arab countries have been flexing their political and religious muscles. Indeed, the hitherto dominant West came to realize that more account would have to be taken of the needs and views of developing countries. Technological advance also brought an awareness that the world is a global village by discovering, for example, that destroying the forests of South America affects the climate of Great Britain. No country could continue to see itself as being fully independent of some reliance on other countries and thus the need arose for a move towards interdependence.

As a consequence, there were significant political realignments. When Britain signed the treaty which would eventually lead to full membership of the European Community, thereby shifting its political gaze more intently towards Europe, the members of Commonwealth countries looked to their immediate neighbours rather than to Britain for economic support and political solidarity. Those countries which did not feel at ease with the East–West alignment brought about by the cold war, moved towards a group of non-aligned nations.

It was the young who had both the room to reflect on the direction that society was moving and the opportunity to protest about it. A number of people showed their disgust by 'dropping out' of society: the alternative culture embodied in the Hippie Movement grew from these times; those who could afford it turned their backs on conventional Western religions and went to the East in search of enlightenment. Protest took to the streets in 1968 when there were student riots in most European capital cities. These disturbing and exciting times were reflected in contemporary popular songs. Bob Dylan in the early 1960s was prophetic in his song, 'The Times They are A-changing'. Peter Seager and Lee Hays expressed the hopes of many in the song 'If I Had a Hammer' with the words:

> I'd hammer out justice, I'd hammer out freedom!
> I'd hammer out love between my brother and my sister
> All over this land.

Fred Dallas expressed similar sentiments in 'The Family of Man', while P. F. Sloan articulated the fears of many about a nuclear holocaust in 'The Eve of Destruction'.

The great upheavals in society were reflected in the various parts of the Church. Dr John Robinson, Bishop of Woolwich, shook the Church establishment in 1963 with the publication of *Honest to God*, in which he stated:

> I believe we are being called, over the years ahead, to far more than a restating of traditional orthodoxy in modern terms. Indeed, if our defence of the Faith is limited to this, we shall

find in all likelihood that we have lost out to all but a tiny religious remnant ... For I am convinced that there is a growing gulf between the traditional orthodox supernaturalism in which our Faith has been framed and the categories which the 'lay' world (for want of a better term) finds meaningful today.[2]

Robinson was saying to the Church establishment what the young were saying to the political establishment, namely that there was an unacceptable gap between those in power and those whom they were supposed to be representing and leading.

The Roman Catholic Church faced one of the biggest upheavals in its history when Pope John XXIII (regarded as a transitional Pope because he was seventy-eight years of age at his election) announced at the end of a prayer service for Church unity on 25 January 1959 his intention to call an Ecumenical Council for the universal Church. The Pope hoped that this Council would be a means of spiritual and apostolic renewal, an updating of the Church in modern times and a service to the unity of the Church. This Second Vatican Council assembled in 1962 and initiated changes affecting every area of Church life upon which the Roman Catholic and wider Church continue to reflect. Of particular significance for our concern is that Latin gave way to the vernacular and the congregation were encouraged to be active liturgically. One way of the congregation being active in the liturgy was through the singing of hymns.

At the same time, the Bible was translated into modern English, with the New Testament of the New English Bible appearing in 1961. Over the last thirty years there have been many new translations into modern English. Main-line churches were facing demands for liturgical renewal and when this was recognized, churches felt it was important not simply to look at the language of the liturgy, but also to look at the theology. One of the fruits of liturgical renewal was an attempt to restore the Eucharist to the place which it held in early Christian practice as the central service of the Church every Sunday. There has been considerable – though certainly not complete – success in this, but it may also be viewed as another way of making the Church less accessible to the non-committed, since only the confirmed are invited to receive Communion.

Clearly, in the United Kingdom, the 1960s was a time when many turned away from the Church. Many would have regarded the Church as an arm of the political establishment and would have expressed their irritation with the one by non-attendance of the other or by attending churches not related to the establishment. Church of England statistics show a dramatic drop in numbers coming forward for confirmation and Easter communicants:[3]

Statistic	Year	Numbers (000s)
Nos confirmed	1940	144
	1950	142
	1960	191
	1970	113

Statistic	Year	Numbers (000s)
Easter Communicants	1940	2156
	1950	2004
	1960	2339
	1970	1814

What was the reaction of the churches to all this? Some, who believed that the primary concern of the Christian faith was a personal salvation and private religion, did not see that events outside Church had any relevance to what happened inside. Others, who understood God's Kingdom as a more corporate entity and believed that what happened inside Church was intricately enmeshed with what happened outside, were taking seriously the challenges and changes and struggled long and hard with issues of faith and society. The World Council of Churches (WCC) was a catalyst to the debates and challenges of the late 1960s and 1970s as it was passing through a particularly active and radical phase, giving, in effect, a theological voice to a number of the issues being raised by those questioning the status quo. For example, the WCC General Assembly at Uppsala in 1968 (the year of the student demonstrations in

European capitals) was the most activist and politically oriented
assembly that had ever met where the youth made it clear that
they were not satisfied with the role given them at the assembly.
Uppsala made special mention of white racism lying at the root
of white denomination and privilege. Two years later the WCC
established the contentious Programme to Combat Racism
which was received so negatively by some member churches
that they resigned from the WCC. In 1973 it asserted that
there was a strong connection between Church and society
when it argued the link between 'the unity of the Church' and
the 'unity of mankind'.

While the WCC was encouraging greater political involvement, two other movements encouraged retreat. First there
was the Charismatic Movement which was so named in 1963.
Originally it viewed the occurrence of Pentecostal experience
within the historic denominations, but by the mid–1970s there
were signs of newly emerging groups of Christians outside the
main-line churches who claimed the same spiritual experience
yet who were clearly not Pentecostals and indeed regarded
themselves as non-denominational. One of the emphases in the
theology of the Charismatic Movement is on the importance
of personal conversion which has, in the past, led to taking
little account of this world in order to concentrate on God.

Second, the 1960s saw the rise of the House Church Movement. It would be misleading to suggest that there is a theology
upon which all House Churches agree, but some general comments can be made. House Churches tend to be charismatic
and non-denominational and their theology draws on an understanding of the Church found in such groups as the Brethren
and a Pentecostal understanding of the Holy Spirit. Many
House Churches regarded themselves as an alternative to main-
line churches whom they believed to have compromised their
interpretation of the Gospel. Like the theology of the Charismatic Movement, House Churches considered social involvement to be unimportant since members concentrated on their
personal relationship with God and with other members of the
House Church.

While some young people turned their backs on the
Church completely and others looked towards the East for their

spirituality, there were a number who wanted to hold on to their Christian faith and yet were searching for a spiritual expression for their inner tumult. A great number found what they were looking for in the ecumenical religious community of Taizé, nestling among the hills of Burgundy in France. The community, under the leadership of Brother Roger was active during the Second World War, but it gained its international fame after 1968 when the great influx of young people discovered that they felt both accepted and heard there.

Having seen, albeit in a cursory way, how the Christian faith has related to changes within society, sometimes by full engagement with society, sometimes by withdrawal, we must now examine how hymns have been theological barometers of change. Hymns have, at various times, reflected, interpreted and challenged both Church and society.

Just as the words of prophets, as they interpret the times, are often appreciated by the majority only long after they have been uttered, so, in the same way, the words of hymn-writers, as they too interpret the times, are sometimes only appreciated long after they are written. For example, Methodist writer Fred Pratt Green wrote in 1947 the hymn 'How Wonderful this World of Thine'. Pratt Green's friend, Revd Francis Westbrook, wanted to include it in a new Sunday School hymn book. However, the Epworth Press argued against the scientific explanation of the origin of the earth mentioned in the second line:

> How wonderful this world of thine,
> A fragment of a fiery sun,
> How lovely and how small!
> Where all things serve thy great design,
> Where life's adventure is begun
> In Thee, the life of all.

Thirty-six years later, when the sentiments seemed dated to Pratt Green, he reluctantly permitted the hymn, with minor alterations, to appear in the Methodist book *Hymns and Psalms*.[4]

The first movement which heralded to the Church a change in the direction of hymns was the Twentieth Century Church Light Music Group. Apart from a few new compositions, this group, made up of clergy and laymen under the direction of

Revd Geoffrey Beaumont (who also composed a Folk Mass), wrote modern, 'popular' tunes to accompany traditional hymn words. In the words of the composers:

> These hymn tunes have been written for congregational worship by 20th century congregations. The styles vary, but they all seek to express in the musical idiom of light music – music which is common to almost everyone – the common worship of the People of God. They are offered in the belief that not only the great and lasting music of the past but also the ordinary and transient music of today – which is the background to the lives of so many – has a rightful place in our worship.
>
> The music is easy to sing, and the piano arrangements should not only be treated freely and with vitality, but may also be adapted for any combination of instruments, including the organ. Drums are also helpful in keeping the rhythm.[5]

'At the Name of Jesus', 'Firmly I Believe and Truly', 'Holy, Holy, Holy, Lord God Almighty', 'Love Divine, All Loves Excelling' and 'O Jesus I Have Promised' are among the hymns to which the group set new tunes. Although the collection of hymns was initially embraced with enthusiasm (there were many reprints of the collection), indicating the deep need for an injection of new life in hymnody, the acclaim was not unaccompanied by severely critical voices. Kenneth Long in *The Music of the English Church* commented that their misguided attempt to get young people into the Church did not work and that they were not professional artists but:

> misguided parsons trying to reproduce the 'pop' styles of their own undergraduate days, dimly remembered. Thus Beaumont's 'Folk Mass' is redolent of the thirties and breathes, perhaps somewhat feebly, the spirit of Fred Astaire and Ginger Rogers: it is naively out of touch with recent styles. Perhaps the most serious criticism of so much of this Twentieth Century 'Light' Music is that it is bad of its kind.[6]

Erik Routley in *The Church and its Music* comments with equal venom:

If early Christians felt that music associated with the theatre unsuitable for use in Christian worship, then music reminiscent of the pantomime (as Geoffrey Beaumont's) certainly is.[7]

None of this music was intended to last. 'Lord Jesus Christ, You Have Come to Us', which was one of the few totally new compositions, has found its way into a number of hymn books and 'At the Name of Jesus' and 'O Jesus I Have Promised' are still occasionally sung, but very few others remain in contemporary repertoires. The Church Light Music Group made the mistake of tinkering and modernizing in the wrong way. The thought of singing hymns in Church to anything other than the organ was too hard for many to contemplate, but the Group's biggest error was to set well-known and well-loved words to new tunes. As we have already seen, a hymn is well known and well loved precisely because of the match of words and tunes. However, despite all of this, the Church Light Music Group fulfilled an important task by showing that congregations were wanting something new and fresh in their hymnody and by preparing the soil for the changes which were to come.

Poet and song-writer Sydney Carter captured the spirit of the times with a directness and freshness. The questioning which John Robinson articulated in *Honest to God* and the need to express a new understanding of the faith in a new idiom was part of Carter's appeal. The title of his book, *Rock of Doubt*, sums up his relationship with conventional religion. Song plays an important part in his expression of faith:

> Song, I saw, was the key; and folk song in particular. Here, for me at any rate, was the spell, the medicine, which I could not understand yet which could heal me all the same. It demanded no impossible belief in God or Jesus or the Virgin Birth; it demanded no political allegiance; it did not seem to care if you were a monk or married, a commando or a pacifist.[8]

These words reveal why Carter appealed both to the young who were disillusioned by institutional religion and those on the edge of faith. 'Lord of the Dance', set to a Shaker tune, injects a sense of joy into the life of Jesus Christ and encourages the singer to join in the cosmic dance. Equating the life of faith with a dance was a new concept for many and unacceptable to some who were suspicious of syncretistic tendencies. Not once is the name of Jesus Christ mentioned in the hymn, yet the subject is abundantly clear. So too are Carter's sympathies: the scribe and the pharisee would not join in the dance, but the fishermen James and John did; it was the 'holy people' who criticized him for healing on the Sabbath and who crucified him. Despite all that they did to him, they could not keep him down because,

> I am the life that'll never, never die;
> I'll live in you if you'll live in me;
> I am the Lord of the Dance, said he.

It is clear that Carter is equating the religious establishment of Jesus' time with the contemporary religious establishment, begging the question as to whether one is better than the other since both appear to crucify the vibrant, living Christ.

Sydney Carter is also able to express the paradoxes and difficulties within the Christian faith which so many felt but feared that voicing them would be disloyal. In 'It was on a Friday Morning', which tells of the events of Good Friday, are the words,

> 'It's God they ought to crucify instead of you and me'
> I said to the carpenter a-hanging on the tree.

'When I Needed a Neighbour' was first published in the early 1960s and reflects the growing public awareness of the needs of many in the developing world as it refers to the 'hungry and thirsty', the 'cold and the naked' and as it relates the need for a 'shelter' and a 'healer'.[9]

Sydney Carter's hymns set to folk tunes live in a category of their own, but at the same time as Carter there emerged a number of writers who concentrated on the Social Gospel. In the late 1960s Congregational Minister Fred Kaan (who spent some time working in Geneva for the World Council of Churches) published a version of the Magnificat. 'Sing We a Song of High Revolt' where, in the last verse we find:

He calls us to revolt and fight.
with him for what is just and right.

This hymn identifies with the powerless and places God on
their side over and against those in power. There can be no
question of the partisan nature of this hymn which is usually
set to the military sounding tune of Cannons which is an adaptation of melody of Handel. There is even less question of its
partisan nature in *Hymns of the City*, published by the Sheffield-
based Urban Theology Unit, where it is sung to the Red Flag.

This concern for the oppressed is a feature of many of Kaan's
hymns: for example, in 'For the Healing of the Nations' are
the lines:

> All that kills abundant living,
> let it from the earth be banned;
> pride of status, race or schooling,
> dogmas that obscure your plan.

And in the harvest hymn 'Now Join We to Praise the Creator':

> But also of need and starvation
> we sing with concern and despair,
> of skills that are used for destruction,
> of land that is burnt and laid bare.[10]

These hymns of Kaan (and many more) have found their way
into the hymn books of main-line churches. Kaan has many
contemporaries writing in similar style including Brian Wren,
Albert Bayly and Fred Pratt Green. Writers who have gained
prominence more recently continue in similar vein as can be
seen in this hymn by John Bell and Graham Maule of the Iona
Community:

Inspired by love and anger, disturbed by need and pain,
Informed of God's own bias, we ask him once again:
'How long must some folk suffer? How long can few folk mind?
How long dare vain self interest turn prayer and pity blind?'

Fred Pratt Green showed his concern for those churches which
responded to the changes and challenges by ignoring them and
becoming over-concerned with their own organization:

When the Church of Jesus
Shuts its outer door,
Lest the roar of traffic
Drown the voice of prayer:
May our prayers, Lord, make us
Ten times more aware
That the world we banish
Is our Christian care.[11]

Contemporary Social Gospel hymns take account of contemporary concerns, as can be seen in another Iona hymn, 'Power Stalks the Earth Both by Purpose and Accident':

Power of computer to file information may
Keep for the few what the many should be told.
Power of the party which governs the nation can
Seldom be challenged and rarely be cajoled.
Look to the one who embraces the frightened folk,
Those more aware of the wrong than of their right;
Learn from the one who will speak for the silenced ones,
Hear for the deaf, and provide the blind with sight.[12]

Fred Pratt Green highlights other contemporary concerns in 'God in his Love for us Lent us this Planet':

From its pollution, misuse, and destruction,
Good Lord, deliver us, world without end![13]

One of the features of this Social Gospel hymn is the direct link between hymn and issue which means that there is little or no reference to the sacred story and a minimal reflection on the great theological themes. It is as though the reflection has been done before the author has put pen to paper and the singers receive the results of the reflection but not its process. This means that the hymns concentrate on how the singers should behave rather than how they relate to God. These hymns rarely mention the Church but make the redemption of society an end in itself. Sung in isolation some would appear to be humanist, but sung in a Church which surrounds the worshipper with visual symbols of the great theological themes (in stained glass, cross and font) and sung in the liturgy which articulates such themes (in Gloria, Creed and Prayer of Thanksgiving), these hymns have the potential of being very powerful.

The Charismatic Movement in the 1960s and 1970s emphasized a personal relationship with God:

> I'm not alone for my Father is with me,
> With me wherever I go . . .
> He's with me, he loves me wherever I go.
>
> Jesus, I love you, Jesus I love you, take my life.

The future in which adherents should put all their trust was certainly not in this world:

> On Jordan's stormy banks I stand and cast a wishful eye
> to Canaan's fair and happy land where my possessions lie.
> I am bound for the promised land.

Meanwhile, this life should be spent with fellow-believers who have been called out of this world, a place of tribulation:

> For we are a chosen race, a royal priesthood, holy
>   nation.
> Once no people, now God's people . . .
> We will serve through tribulation,
> we will follow to the cross.

All these hymns encourage withdrawal from this world into the community of God's Chosen in order to ensure that personal relationship with God which will be fulfilled in the next world. The more classical hymns which are sung are selected because they provide an acceptable theological emphasis. For example, 'Guide Me, O Thou Great Jehovah' describes the world as a 'barren land'. Harry Emerson Fosdick's hymn 'God of Grace and God of Glory' recognizes God's Chosen as living in a sea of evil:

> Lo! the hosts of evil round us
> Scorn thy Christ, assail his ways![14]

Hymns addressed to the Deity tend to call upon the second person of the Trinity, Jesus Christ. The immediacy and intimacy with God that this engenders removes the need for somebody to mediate between worshipper and God who is not far off, but nearby. The result of this emphasis is that the hierarchy of the main-line Churches as seen in their priests and ministers is considered unnecessary. Members of House Churches share this approach to God which they believe renders an ordained ministry unnecessary.

The Christian Community of Taizé, already mentioned, encouraged people to discover God at work within themselves and in the wider world. Taizé was (and is) a spiritual magnet to many thousands of young people from all over the world. Although the vast majority of pilgrims to Taizé are young, people of all ages are to be found there. Taizé was known as a place of liturgical experimentation in the 1950s, but one of the dilemmas it faced was that music which suited the community was difficult for visitors. This vexed Brother Roger, the community leader, who felt that it was important to be open to new ways and to the needs of visitors. One night in the 1970s, the community were singing the response to Psalm 27, 'Le Seigneur est ma lumière et mon salut' ('The Lord is my light and my salvation'), when they discovered that frequent repetition was effective. From this developed the repetitive singing for which Taizé is internationally known. Musician Jacques Berthier has composed 90 percent of the music which is set to responses taken from psalms in particular, Scripture in general, elements of the liturgy and some prayers of Brother Roger. The words are, for the most part, few and simple so that different language groups can understand and sing them easily. Thus:

Cantate Domino, Alleluia, Alleluia, Jubilate Deo.
(Sing praises to the Lord, Alleluia! Sing in joy and gladness)

Bleibet hier und wachet mit mir. Wachet und betet, wachet und betet.
(Stay here and watch with me. Watch and pray, watch and pray)

Ubi caritas et amor, ubi caritas Deus ibi est.

(Living charity and steadfast love, living charity shows
the heart of God)

El Senyor es la meva forca, el Senyor el meucant. Ell
  m'ha estat la salvacio. En ell confio i no tinc por, en
  ell confio i no tinc por.
(In the Lord I'll ever be thankful, in the Lord I will
  rejoice. Look to God, do not be afraid, lift up your
  voices the Lord is near; lift up your voices the Lord is
  near)

How blest are those who are poor, the Kingdom of God
is near.[15]

As people from different parts of the world hear their own
languages being used in the worship of God, they know that
their own culture and background are being taken seriously.
As people worship God in languages other than their own,
they enter into a deeper solidarity with their new friends from
other parts of the world. Song and silence (two aspects common
to all humanity) make up a large part of the worship in the
Church of Reconciliation at Taizé. The words of the hymns are
intended to open up the singers to God. The tunes are as
simple as the words, containing the resonances of Gregorian
chant. The simplicity of the words and of the music is enhanced
by the atmosphere of the church building in which the worshippers sit on the floor to share in a spirituality of considerable
depth.

Although the Taizé hymns are simple and short, a great deal
can be gleaned from them about the theology which underpins
the community. First, the fact that they are written in so many
languages indicates an all-embracing, inclusive understanding
of the Christian faith. Secondly, there is a concern for those who
are marginalized by society, as the last hymn above indicates,
regardless of whether they are believers or not. Thirdly, these
hymns show how it is important for individuals to have the
freedom to grow and develop in the way that God intended.
All the hymns are praising God or petition for God to be
present: none of them tells the singers how they should behave.

It would have been this total acceptance by the community (and, through implication, by God) that would have attracted young people to Taizé in the first place. It is not surprising that with the destruction of the Berlin Wall, Taizé has become a place of pilgrimage for many young people from Eastern Europe.

Iona Abbey, situated off the west coast of Scotland, also has a special appeal to young people. St Columba is said to have landed on Iona with his twelve followers on the eve of Pentecost 563 and established the Iona Community. In 1938 George MacLeod, a Church of Scotland Minister, landed on Iona to build a new Iona Community whose task would be to train Church of Scotland ministers for ministry in the new urban Scotland. At its heart, MacLeod was wanting this new community to take seriously the challenges for mission thrown before the Church which was tending to preach an individual salvation ignoring the deep-rooted problems of the corporate world. He was wanting to recapture the enthusiasm of the early Celtic Church to infuse every area of life with the Christian spirit. Iona today, which has members both on the island, in community houses in industrial Glasgow and throughout the world, attracts many pilgrims to its vision of peace (pacifism is part of its rule), its ministry of welcome and its commitment to asking radical questions from its strong Celtic Christian roots about the environment and the direction in which society is moving. The whole nuclear threat (especially with nuclear submarines based in Scottish waters) and the ecological question have been of particular concern.

The 1980s saw a renewed interest in the worship of the Iona community where the historical and ecumenical dimensions of the island were combined with contemporary concerns. These concerns were given voice in hymns through the talents of John Bell and Graham Maule.

Celtic Christianity affirms the world and sees God at work in the simple and ordinary. Mary is not regarded as the high queen of heaven but as a simple country girl; Peter is not considered as an ecclesiastic but as a fisherman sharing his joys and sorrows; Jesus is first and foremost acknowledged as a person to whom ordinary people can relate. Many of these

themes are gathered up in 'Praise to the Lord for the Joys of
the Earth':

> Praise to the Lord for the joys of the earth:
> Cycles of season and reason and birth,
> Contrasts in outlook and landscape and need,
> Challenge of famine, pollution and greed.
>
> Praise to the Lord for the carpenter's son,
> Dovetailing worship and work into one:
> Tradesman and teacher and vagrant and friend,
> Source of all life in this world without end.

The themes of forgiveness and self-acceptance are strong and
frequent, as can be seen in 'Will You Come and Follow Me?':

> Will you love the 'you' you hide
> If I but call your name?
> Will you quell the fear inside
> And never be the same?
> Will you use the faith you've found
> To reshape the world around,
> Through my sight and touch and sound
> In you and you in me?

The challenge of involvement is strong:

> Don't tell me of a faith that fears
> To face the world around;
> Don't dull my mind with easy thoughts
> Of grace without a ground.
>
> Don't speak of piety and prayers
> Absolved from human need:
> Don't talk of spirit without flesh
> Like harvest without seed.
>
> So let the Gospel come alive,
> In actions plain to see
> In imitation of the one
> Whose love extends to me.

One of the geniuses of the Iona hymns is how the type of tune used often matches the sentiment of the hymn. So, 'No One Will Ever be the Same', where encouragement is given to those who feel dispossessed, is set to a tune in the style of a Negro Spiritual. When one remembers that these Spirituals were freedom songs one is aware of the power that the tune invests in the words:

We're going to shine like the sun in the Kingdom of Heaven,
Shine like the sun in the Kingdom of Heaven;
We're going to shine like the sun in the Kingdom of Heaven
And no one will ever be the same.

Chorus: And it's all in Jesus' name . . .
That no one will ever be the same.

We're going to learn from the poor in the Kingdom of Heaven . . .

We're going to walk with the weak in the Kingdom of
    Heaven . . .
And it all starts now in the Kingdom of Heaven.[16]

We now turn to the hymns of Graham Kendrick, one of our most prolific contemporary hymn-writers. Though he has links with the House Church Movement, Kendrick's background is ecumenical. The changing theological emphasis in his hymns in the 1980s is an indication of a consensus which has developed among churches during that particular decade. House Churches, formerly fiercely independent, are now more involved in interchurch relations and some are concerned with social involvement.

The frequent occurrence of such references to the Church as made up of the 'clean', who have been cleansed by Christ's 'blood' and who are fighting against the powers of 'darkness' is an indication that the Church views its members as God's Chosen and Elect.[17] In the early 1980s Kendrick writes about the importance of building up God's Church:

God is at work in us
His purpose to perform,

> Building a kingdom
> Of power not of words,
> Where things impossible
> By faith shall be made possible.

And

> Restore, O Lord,
> In all the earth Your fame,
> And in our time revive
> The church that bears Your name.

Within the Church adherents are encouraged to follow the example of the 'Servant King' and to learn 'How to serve', whereas the imagery changes for engagement outside:

> Magnificent Warrior,
> We hear Your strong command
> To join the ranks of light
> And march into the fight.

In later hymns concern for the suffering is expressed:

> O Lord, while precious children starve
> The tools of war increase;
> Their bread is broken.

The answer is:

> Revive Your church again.
> Let justice flow like rivers
> And righteousness like a never failing stream.

The major difference between the emphases of Kendrick and the Social Gospel hymns of Kaan, Pratt Green and Wren, is that Kendrick equates the Kingdom with the Church into which the poor and, indeed, the whole nation are encouraged. The former group, on the other hand, feel that the Church should be the instrument by which the marginalized are lifted up but there is no precondition about joining since the Kingdom is bigger than the Church. Nevertheless, the significant point is that the House Church is taking seriously social and political issues in the middle and late 1980s.[18]

In the 1980s main-line churches became more open to some of the fruits of Charismatic Renewal and so, many who left churches which did not acknowledge renewal have returned, challenged and revitalized, to their former spiritual homes. The Renewal Movement and House Church share many of the same hymns (certainly Graham Kendrick is a favourite of both) and many of the same theological emphases. In the hymn book compiled for the Thirteenth National Conference of Anglican Renewal Ministries which met at Swanwick in Derbyshire in 1993, eleven of the fifty-three hymns were written by Graham Kendrick. A few hymns emphasized the need to go out and become engaged with the world, for example:

> There's a hunger deep within our hearts
> To see healing in our nation . . .
> Heal our nation! Heal our nation! . . .
> Bringing justice and forgiveness.[19]

The late 1980s and early 1990s have seen a great sharing of spiritual treasures and insights in the way that various traditions have shared each other's hymns. In the recently published *Baptist Praise and Worship* (1991) and the United Reformed Church's *Rejoice and Sing* (1991) we find, alongside the traditional, hymns from Taizé, Iona, Graham Kendrick and the Renewal Movement. Since the Anglican *Ancient and Modern New Standard* (1983) appeared too early to include hymns which have only recently been sung across such a wide denominational spectrum, it has published the *Ancient and Modern Worship Songs* (1992) to make up for this lack.

Does this sharing of hymns across the denominational divide point towards a closer ecumenical sharing? Do we detect an answer to the prayer in St John's Gospel:

> May they all be one. Father, may they be one in us, as you are in me and I am in you, so that the world may believe it was you who sent me (17.20–1)?

Ecumenism has made great strides forward this century as recent schemes for unity and intercommunion and the formation of councils of churches testify. But ecumenism is more than healing rifts between churches, it is more than churches being able to speak to one another and act together. The ecumenical question needs to be seen within the perspective of society as a whole and the efficacy of churches in their ecumenical endeavours has to be judged from the healing which churches enable within society. The euphoria at the tearing down of the Berlin Wall only temporarily masked other deep divisions which have subsequently surfaced. Indeed, the real divisions between churches reflect the major divisions in our world. John D. Davies, Bishop of Shrewsbury, who has much experience in serving the Church abroad as well as in this country, highlights the dilemma in these prophetic words:

> The old [ecumenical question] was, 'Can the non-episcopally confirmed share in communion with those who are episcopally confirmed?' The new question is 'Can the poor share in communion with those who make them poor?'[20]

6

Hymns Within Worship

Somehow, about forty per cent of churchgoers seem to have picked up the idea that 'singing in churches is for singers.' The truth is that 'singing is for believers.' The relevant question is not 'Do you have a voice?' but, 'Do you have a song?'

David Hustad

When discussing the possibility of a mid-week 'said' service of Holy Communion in the Copperbelt town of Northern Zambia, I was told quite firmly by a young Zambian, 'It is not possible to worship Almighty God without singing'. This comment reflects a spirituality which seeks to take every opportunity of engaging with God as fully as possible on every occasion. It also reflects a theology which believes that in our singing we are transported to heaven when our corporate praises are united with those of the whole company of heaven as we join in the worship of God:

> The strains of all its [heaven's] holy throng
> With ours today are blending.[1]

The singing of hymns in worship can reinforce the reality of the One about whom we sing and can transport us beyond ourselves, thereby lifting the whole worship: but so much depends upon the person responsible for making the music. For just as worship can be lifted by our musicians, so too it can be sunk by them. It is not our task to comment on the place of organs and music groups except to say that any instruments in the right hands can be of great benefit, just as any instruments in the wrong hands can be disastrous. What is of significance is that the primary task of the person performing the music is to *listen*, and the secondary task is to play. The musician needs to listen to the prayers and sermon, sense the mood of the congregation, be aware of what is being celebrated and respond appropriately in the accompaniment. There are times when the way that a hymn is played adds the sparkle to a service that is already glowing. If there is a need for musicians to listen, then there has to be something worth hearing, which quite rightly places heavy responsibilities upon the person leading the worship. Inspired preaching can encourage inspired playing which, in turn, can encourage more inspired preaching. When one is constantly lacklustre, the other frequently follows and so the downward spiral begins.

The very act of standing, facing the same direction and singing the same hymn reinforces the unity and corporate identity of the congregation. There may be many areas of Church life where members differ and disagree, but if they are willing to be united in praise of their Creator then maybe their areas of disagreement should be seen as part of the rich diversity that needs to be encouraged rather than subjugated. Having said this, the Christian Community in song can sometimes sound like a battle-field as people vie with each other in volume, speed and length of notes at the beginning and end of verses. Again, if the community can listen to each other in song, then this will probably spill over into other areas of life, both in and out of Church. If the community can sing prayerfully, then its members will be helped to pray both corporately and individually.

As well as cementing a diverse community, the hymn, through its various expressions, enables such unity to be a comfort, support and sign of hope at times of adversity. For example, Christian Communities of Black South Africans were given hope with the hymn 'Siyahamba':

> We are marching in the light of God,
> We are marching in the light of God.[2]

Hymn-singing can also be an act of unity between congregations of different denominations, thereby fulfilling an ecumenical function. A Roman Catholic and Methodist may not be able to share in Holy Communion, and there may be some prayers in which they cannot share, but they would be able to stand and sing many hymns together.

Hymns have the power of earthing worship in the experience of the congregation. For example, a service and sermon concentrating on the Creator God may be earthed for a congregation with the words:

> Lord of beauty, thine the splendour
> shewn in earth and sky and sea,
> burning sun and moonlight tender,
> hill and river, flower and tree:
> lest we fail our praise to render
> touch our eyes that they may see.[3]

Hymns can sharpen our missionary calling, as in the hymn 'God of Freedom, God of Justice', written by Shirley Murray for Amnesty International. The last verse reads:

> Make in us a captive conscience
> quick to hear, to act, to plead;
> make us truly sisters, brothers,
> of whatever race or creed;
> teach us to be fully human,
> open to each other's need.[4]

Although many hymns are 'shared' by denominations, nevertheless, different denominations use hymns in different ways. So, Wesley's hymn 'Love Divine, All Loves Excelling' will fulfil a different function in an Anglican service from what it would in a Methodist service.[5] We now move on to explore how different traditions use hymns and why they are used in their particular way. We go on to consider the significance of *Mission Praise*, then we look at hymns in schools. Finally we consider the power of those who select hymns and those who edit them. Hymn books themselves provide the best clues.

Hymns in the Anglican Tradition

In his book, *The Hymns of Wesley and Watts*, devoted Congregationalist Bernard Manning highlights the different function of hymns:

Hymns are for us Dissenters what the liturgy is for the Anglican. They are the framework, the setting, the conventional, the traditional part of divine service as we use it.[6]

Hymns were forced on Anglicans comparatively late because the establishment viewed them with suspicion. All that was necessary for belief could be found within the pages of the Book of Common Prayer and the Bible. Indeed there is no provision at all for hymns in the 1662 Prayer Book with one exception, namely that the hymn/prayer 'Veni Creator Spiritus' ('Come Holy Ghost') can be found in the Ordination of Priests and the Consecration of Bishops. This refusal by the Book of Common Prayer to acknowledge hymns is not surprising when one remembers that hymn-singing was not widely accepted by Anglicans until well into the nineteenth century.

There has never been an official hymn book of the Church of England, but the book that was seriously considered for this task was *Hymns Ancient and Modern*, first published in 1861. Although not the first hymn book to order its hymns according to the Church's year, it set a pattern which gave hymns an importance and emphasis for which Anglicans were grasping. It acknowledges the place of the Prayer Book and arranges its hymns according to the liturgical seasons. Its first section is devoted to times (morning, evening, days of the week) and the Christian year (Advent, Christmas, Epiphany and so on). There is a large section devoted to general hymns where the arrangement begins with the Holy Trinity and then the persons of the Trinity, followed by the Church and a section on the Christian life. This arrangement has, by and large, been followed at the major revisions of the book, including its latest in 1983. As we have seen, one of the reasons for the great and unexpected success of the 1861 *Hymns Ancient and Modern* was that, although it was adventurous in some of the hymns it included, its editors, who were mainly country parish priests, consulted widely about the popularity and acceptability of hymns. The 1983 edition draws attention to the popular nature of hymn books in its Preface:

> A good hymn-book is necessarily an endeavour in high democracy. The lifetime of a hymn is one which congregations decide by an unconscious process.[7]

The *English Hymnal* (first published in 1906) organizes its contents in a similar way to *Hymns Ancient and Modern* thereby reinforcing the tradition of hymns as accompaniments to the liturgy. The *English Hymnal* was published at a time when Anglo-Catholicism was becoming more open and confident and was designed for Churches with Mass and plainsong. The book also attempts to relate Catholic spirituality to cultural context in that many hymns were set to traditional folk tunes: so we find 'O Little Town of Bethlehem' set to Forest Green, 'Father Hear the Prayer We Offer', to Sussex and 'Firmly I Believe and Truly' to the Warwickshire ballad Shipston. This use of folk tunes also contained an element of folk revivalism, wanting to preserve a tradition that was in danger of being lost. Ralph Vaughan Williams, a member of its distinguished editorial team, was responsible for these adaptations. The *New English Hymnal*, published in 1986, succeeded the 1906 edition, retaining approximately four hundred of the original 656 hymns. The Preface confirms the place of hymns in Anglican worship:

> We have retained the general arrangement of the English Hymnal, based chiefly on the Church's year and her sacramental life. In a book whose primary purpose is to be an accompaniment to the liturgy there was no reason to do otherwise.[8]

One hymn book which has had more influence than is generally acknowledged is *Songs of Praise*. First published in 1925 it was devised for use by bodies outside as well as inside the Church, in particular it was hoped that the book would be used by schools. As we shall see, this latter hope was successfully realized. Although not specifically written for the Church of England, it is predominantly Anglican in ethos. The book was compiled to be national in character with a number of vigorous tunes and fine, strong poems. The Preface to the Enlarged Edition states:

> our advisers and we ourselves have born well in mind the fact that our churches, both Anglican and Free Church, have alienated during the last half-century much of the strongest character and intelligence of the Nation by the use of weak

verse and music, and that the process of attraction or repulsion takes place every time a service is held.

As will be gathered from such statements, it is a 'hearty' hymn book with upper-middle-class sentiments:

> We thank thee for games, and for friendship and fun,
> And the strength in our limbs when we wrestle and run,
> And all that is good and delightful and true.

Kenneth Long in *The Music of the English Church* felt that *Songs of Praise* was aggressively typical of the 1920s and felt it was well described in the slogan 'Praise the Lord and Pass the Ammunition'.[9] Its value for school use is well illustrated in this hymn which praises God for the great seers who have 'led the van, truth writ upon their banners'. The first such seer named is Amos and then in the third verse we find:

> For Socrates who, phrase by phrase,
> Talked men to truth, unshrinking,
> And left for Plato's mighty grace
> To mould our ways of thinking.[10]

Although the arrangement of hymns in *Songs of Praise* is similar to *Hymns Ancient and Modern* and *English Hymnal*, it is clear that the intention of its compilers was to remove some of the sentimentality out of religion and make the Christian faith more accessible and acceptable to the uncommitted. In the attempt to make Christian imagery relevant, it sometimes eviscerated it. The first verse of 'Christian, Dost Thou See Them?' in *Hymns Ancient and Modern* reads:

> Christian, up and smite them,
> Counting gain but loss;
> Smite them by the merit
> Of the holy Cross . . . ,

but is changed in *Songs of Praise* to:

> Christian up, and follow;
> His the perfect school,
> Learn to make men happy
> By the Golden Rule.

Hymns which accompany the liturgy are freed from the demands of needing to make strong explicit doctrinal statements and so they can be aids to devotion and personal piety. Accordingly, it is possible for a congregation to reflect on the Eucharist through their emotions and sentiments in a hymn in the knowledge that a Eucharistic theology is enshrined in the liturgy. The hymn 'Sweet Sacrament Divine' may not express a commonly held view of the Eucharist as it refers to the adoration of the sacrament, but in a service authorized for Anglicans as a whole, it expresses a view of the sacrament helpful to some:

> Sweet Sacrament divine,
> hid in thine earthly home,
> lo, round thy lowly shrine,
> with suppliant hearts we come;
> Jesu, to thee our voice we raise
> in songs of love and heartfelt praise:
> Sweet Sacrament divine.[11]

When the liturgy speaks of God the Creator, it is possible for a congregation to emphasize the events of harvest and to muse on how this is related to the Second Coming, as in Henry Alford's hymn:

> Come, ye thankful people, come,
> raise the song of harvest-home!
> All be safely gathered in,
> Ere the winter storms begin;
> God, our Maker, doth provide
> for our wants to be supplied;
> come to God's own temple, come;
> raise the song of harvest-home!
>
> For the Lord our God shall come,
> and shall take his harvest home;
> from his field shall purge away
> all that doth offend, that day;
> give his angels charge at last
> in the fire the tares to cast,

> but the fruitful ears to store
> in his garner evermore.[12]

There are, of course, many hymns in Anglican hymn books which make doctrinal statements, but, again, such statements are not the primary purpose of hymns in a church with a strong liturgy.

Hymns in the Baptist Tradition

Benjamin Keach (1640–1704) minister of Horsley-down Baptist Church in Southwark, was a prolific hymn-writer. In due course, he persuaded his congregation to accept the New Testament pattern of singing a hymn at the close of the Lord's Supper. Eventually his congregation sang a hymn at every service, but at the end so that objectors could withdraw if they wished. This information enables us to appreciate a Baptist approach to hymns, which is far from unified. Baptists are heirs of the Reformation with its tradition of music and song and they are also heirs of a Puritan tradition which, at its most liberal, was very suspicious towards music in worship, (just about allowing the metrical psalms to be sung) and, at its most conservative, rejected it altogether. Strong in the Baptist tradition is the supreme authority of Scripture which accounts for the metrical psalms being allowed by some of the more liberal puritans. There has traditionally been a reluctance for Baptists to be dependent on hymns for their theology, thus making them closer to an Anglican rather than Methodist usage. Also, the fact that there has not been a major Baptist hymn-writer provides a clue to the place of hymns in the Baptist tradition. In *Singing the Faith*, a book of essays by members of the Joint Liturgical Group on the use of hymns in the liturgy, Neville Clark, Principal of South Wales Baptist College, writes in a chapter on the use of Baptist hymns in churches:

> From first to last, music has remained in a real sense incidental to corporate worship. Arguably, its ranking current functions are masking, backing, and mood creating. It covers entry, withdrawal, or necessary movement. It supports singing, it strikes

a suitable note by assisting feeling tones. Nor is this surprising. For its originating traditions have always pressed Baptist worship in the direction of the declaratory and didactic mould. The Word of God is to be spoken and heard. Music is seldom far away from other components of corporate worship in being viewed as an adjunct to the sermon; for worship is seen as essentially concerned with a receiving rather than with an offering, with divine approach rather than with human response, with Bach in addressing music to the congregation rather than with Palestrina in addressing music to God.[13]

Others would want to use hymns to construct the liturgy as the recently published *Baptist Praise and Worship* reveals. Published in 1992, this hymn book views hymns as the liturgy of the people, almost taking the place of responses in Prayer Book Services. *Baptist Praise and Worship* has been devised with the hymns arranged around the liturgy with the first section outlining elements that would make up a service: Gathering for Worship, Praise, Invocation and Confession, the Word, Blessing and Dismissal; and the other sections taking in areas of Christian life: Proclaiming the Gospel, Celebrating the Gospel and Living the Gospel. The book is true to its heritage in that there is a section with hymns in Welsh as well as a section with psalms. Also reflected is the Baptist tradition which inclines towards biblically based hymns: indeed, this is one of the only contemporary books which provides a large number of hymns with the Biblical passage which inspired them. So, under the hymn 'Jesus Lives! Your Terrors Now Can, O Death, No More Appal Us', we are informed it is based on Romans 8.11. Timothy Dudley-Smith's hymn, 'Born by the Holy Spirit's Breath' is based on Romans 8 and 'There is a Land of Pure Delight' is based on Deuteronomy 34.

Personal evangelism and personal experience are strong in the Baptist tradition and these elements are not lost in *Baptist Praise and Worship*. Old favourites like Frances Van Alstyne's 'Blessed Assurance, Jesus is Mine' and Robert Walmsley's 'Come Let Us Sing of a Wonderful Love' sit alongside John Bell's 'Come with Me, Come Wander, Come Welcome the World' and Bob Kilpatrick's 'In my Life, Lord, be Glorified, be Glorified'. The recently written hymn 'Cradle, O Lord, in your Arms Everlasting' shows how Baptists can foster very fine hymns of experience. This particular hymn was written by a teacher after a road crash involving school families resulting in the tragic death of one pupil. The tune, Melissa, was named after the pupil who died:

> Cradle, O Lord, in your arms everlasting,
> one that we love and for whom we now pray:
> graces and gifts which in *him* we acknowledge
> comes from the God who rules both night and day.

Hymns in the Methodist Tradition

In the Preface to *A Collection of Hymns for the Use of People called Methodists*, John Wesley writes,

> These hymns are not carelessly jumbled together, but carefully ranged under proper heads, according to the experience of real Christians. So that this book is in effect a little body of experimental and practical divinity.[14]

From the beginning hymns have had an overtly didactic function for Methodists. Indeed, although it is the first four volumes of John Wesley's *Sermons* with the *Notes on the New Testament* which provide the official doctrinal standards for Methodism, nevertheless, the hymns of Charles Wesley are the source of theology for the majority of Methodists. It needs to be remembered that Charles Wesley did not write hymns for a Church but for the Methodist Movement which met at times outside the 'Divine Service' of the Established Church so that members could attend both Movement and Church.

In the past, Methodist worship has been expressed through hymns rather than other forms. If a hymn expresses an act of adoration, then there would be no need for a further expression of that element in the prayers. It would indeed be difficult to better an act of adoration based on George Herbert's hymn 'King of Glory, King of Peace' set for adoration and worship in the *Methodist Hymn Book*:

> King of glory, King of peace,
> I will love Thee;

> and that love may never cease,
> I will move Thee.
> Thou has granted my request,
> Thou hast heard me;
> Thou didst note my working breast,
> Thou has spared me.[15]

If a hymn is a paraphrase of Scripture, then there would be no need to read that particular passage of Scripture. So, William Kethe's 'All People that on Earth do Dwell', would be sung instead of saying Psalm 100:

> All people that on earth do dwell,
> sing to the Lord with cheerful voice:
> Him serve with mirth, his praise forth tell;
> come ye before him and rejoice.[16]

By enabling the congregation to join in the enunciation of adoration and Scripture at key points in services, hymns have not only made the adoration and Scripture impress themselves deeply within the congregation but have also asserted that it is the task of the congregation as well as the minister to adore God and proclaim the Scriptures. Hymns, then, have traditionally held a central position in worship for Methodists and this is reflected by the fact that the Methodist Conference (the governing body for Methodists) authorizes hymn books for Methodists.

Latterly there has been a subtle shift in the way that Methodists have used their hymns. With the publication of the *Methodist Service Book* (1975), the 'Sunday Service' and the 'Sunday Service without the Lord's Supper' have taken a shape similar to those of other churches and although hymns take a major role within the worship, it is arguably not as central as in times past. Hymns are now used more to accompany the worship than to lead it.

Hymns in the United Reformed Church

English and Welsh Congregationalism, the Presbyterian Church of England and the Churches of Christ bring to the relatively recently constituted United Reformed Church (URC) a tradition in which hymns have been the main way that music has been used in worship. A tradition which boasts Isaac Watts as a forefather would naturally give a high priority to hymns. The way in which the URC hymn book, *Rejoice and Sing*, was put together reveals the place of hymns in that tradition. The General Assembly of the URC appointed an Editorial Committee to compile the book. Great care was taken to ensure that the Committee was truly representative of the Church: not just hymnologists and clergy, but lay women and men. The Committee then asked each 'church' which was part of the URC to submit a list of hymns from which the editors made a selection. The editors then published in the URC magazine a list of the hymns they intended using and responses and reactions to the list were invited. Theological emphases were discussed and agreed among the editors, although the General Assembly had asked that they adhere to theological emphases current in their Church. Thus, inclusive language was used wherever possible, though where the original poetry would have been destroyed by any change, the old language remains. For example in Timothy Rees' hymn, 'God is Love: Let Heaven Adore Him', verse 3 is changed from

> God is love: and though with blindness
> sin afflicts the souls of men
> God's eternal loving-kindness
> holds and guides them even then . . .

to

> God is love: and though with blindness
> sin afflicts and clouds the will,
> God's eternal loving-kindness
> holds us fast and guides us still.[17]

Militarism was removed (out goes 'Onward Christian Soldiers!') as was imagery which was considered sentimental and inappropriate as in the second verse of 'Away in the Manger':

> The cattle are lowing the baby awakes,
> but little Lord Jesus no crying he makes.

> I love thee Lord Jesus! Look down from the sky
> and stay by my side until morning is nigh.[18]

Like its contemporaries, this book reflects a changing understanding of mission. There is a move away from the idea of the 'civilized Christian' West bringing civilization and the Gospel to the heathens and there are more hymns on justice and peace. So we no longer find, 'From Greenland's Icy Mountains' with its lines,

> From Greenland's icy mountains,
> From India's coral strand,
> Where Afric's sunny fountains
> Roll down their golden sand,
> From many an ancient river,
> From many a palmy plain,
> They call us to deliver
> Their land from error's chain,[19]

but instead there is 'We Pray for Peace' with the words:

> We pray for peace,
> and not the evil peace
> defending unjust laws
> and nursing prejudice,
> but for the real peace
> of justice, mercy, truth and love.[20]

There remains a number of hymns which look forward to the coming of God's Kingdom and the spreading of the Gospel throughout the world, as in 'Thy Kingdom Come O God'.

There is a vigorous section on baptism and confirmation (seventeen hymns as compared to four in the *Congregational Hymnal* – this latter book, has no hymns specifically on confirmation) and on the Lord's Supper (thirty hymns as compared to twenty-five in the *Congregational Hymnal*). This reflects the influence of the World Council of Churches' Lima Document 'Baptism, Eucharist and Ministry' and the need to incorporate the Churches of Christ theology that baptism should be available for believers as well as children.[21]

Rejoice and Sing structures its hymns in a doctrinal (as compared to a liturgical) sequence, beginning with One God in Trinity, then hymns on the three persons of the Trinity (God the Creator, God Incarnate and God the Life-Giver), the World (entitled Creation's Response to God's Love) and finally the Fulfilled Kingdom (All One in God's Praise). There is no longer a section for harvest, marriage or funerals following a decision to incorporate them in the wider contexts of God's world, Christian living and Easter and Communion of Saints. This ensures that death is not seen in isolation from resurrection and the saints, that marriage is not seen in isolation from the wider Christian family and harvest is not seen in isolation from all of God's gifts and bounty.

Perhaps of all the churches which have revised their hymnaries, the URC's revision is the most radical because of its reconstitution in 1972. But the tradition which gave birth to Isaac Watts continues to produce hymn-writers and hymnologists of distinction, among whom are Erik Routley, Fred Kaan, Albert Bayly and Brian Wren, thereby confirming the continuing significance of hymns in this particular tradition.

Hymns in the Roman Catholic Church

Of all the main-line churches and traditions in England, hymns as part of the major acts of worship have come the latest to Roman Catholics. The Roman Catholic Church has a long and noble tradition of liturgical music, which has been performed by specialists on behalf of the worshippers, leaving the worshippers to listen but not actively to participate. Indeed, although the music was composed for the Mass and to the glory of God, it was often more of a performance and was not liturgical in the proper sense, certainly out of the range of the average congregation. At the beginning of this century Pope Pius X emphasized the fact that sacred music was an integral rather than an extra part of the liturgy and he indicated that Gregorian Chant was the supreme model for sacred music. Although there was, as a result of this, some lay participation in the singing, it was limited.

Hymns may not have been sung at Mass, but they certainly were sung at 'popular devotions' such as the Benediction of the

Blessed Sacrament and the recitation of the Rosary. It was here that the laity had an opportunity of singing in the vernacular such hymns as 'Anima Christi' ('Soul of my Saviour') which was held to be so important in the devotional lives of many Catholics:

> Soul of my Saviour, sanctify my breast;
> Body of Christ, be thou my saving guest;
> Blood of my Saviour, bathe me in thy tide,
> Wash me with water flowing from thy side.[22]

It was the Second Vatican Council in 1962 which heralded a change in the attitude of the Roman Catholic Church towards hymns when it demanded a full and active part in the liturgy by the laity. This was later spelt out more specifically as the laity participating in song when the unity of hearts is more profoundly achieved with the unity of voices.[23]

The Roman Catholic Church has had a lot of work to do and a number of hymn books and writers have made great strides forwards. At first, primarily the hymns used at Catholic devotions were used, but latterly there has been much borrowing from other traditions. Thus looking in the *New Catholic Hymnal* (1971), we find 'All People that on Earth do Dwell', 'O God, Our Help in Ages Past' and 'King of Glory, King of Peace' as well as 'Queen of Mercy, Virgin Mary'. In the Foreword to the book, John Heenan, Cardinal Archbishop of Westminster, writes:

> Fortunately the ecumenical climate allows us to borrow melodies from those other Christian Churches which have always praised God in the English tongue. Catholics are already at home with the splendid hymns traditionally and beautifully sung by Anglican and Non-conformist congregations.
>
> The editors of this Catholic Hymnal have not hesitated to borrow from non-Catholic sources. But they have not been content merely to borrow.[24]

Although many of the hymns have been borrowed, there are a few songs of protest creeping in as well as compositions by contemporary composers. This tendency was continued in *Celebration Hymnal*, published in 1978. There were such classics as 'Abide with Me', 'Crown Him with Many Crowns' and 'Firmly I Believe and Truly', but beside these were hymns from a popular folk tradition such as 'Go, Tell it on the Mountain', 'Gonna Lay Down my Sword and Shield', 'Morning has Broken' and 'Lord of the Dance' as well as Catholic traditionals such as 'Hail Queen of Heav'n'.

Volume 2 of *Celebration Hymnal*, published in 1981, reveals the influence of the Charismatic Movement in such hymns as:

> Jesus, you are my salvation
> Jesus, you're my inspiration
> Jesus, you're the treasure of my life

and

> Lamb of God, Lamb of God
> You take away the sins of the world, the sins of the
>   world.
> Have mercy, have mercy on us.

The latter hymn has the instructions beside it 'Repeat as often as necessary'.[25] This book also contains hymns reflecting the Social Gospel such as Doreen Potter's and Fred Kaan's 'Help Us Accept Each Other as Christ Accepted Us'.

In *New Songs of Celebration* (1989), which is both a second supplement to the *Celebration Hymnal* and an independent collection in its own right, we find more of a distinctive character emerging. The hymns are arranged in alphabetical order, but the index orders hymns under three major headings indicating the theological priorities of the editor which he believes reflects those of the Church. First, there is the Eucharist, secondly the times and seasons of the liturgical year and finally there is a topical index with headings such as Commitment, Church, Creation, Evangelism and Faith. There is a whole section of the book centred upon the Divine Office, reflecting the interest in reviving the services of Morning and Evening Prayer. The collection contains a number of well-known hymnwriters such as Fred Kaan, Timothy Dudley-Smith and Fanny Crosby but the majority are by writers relatively unknown outside the Roman Catholic world signalling an attempt to create a new Catholic identity in hymns.

In many instances, the hymn is the basic musical form in which parts of the liturgy are sung, so, for instance, we find the Gloria (Glory to God in the highest), the Sanctus (Holy, Holy, Holy Lord, God of power and might) and Agnus Dei (Lamb of God, you take away the sins of the world) sung to what sound like hymn tunes. Although this enables a large part of the congregation to participate in the singing, it is at the expense of the variety of musical styles reflecting the kaleidoscope of humanity which can be offered to God in worship. Set alongside the history of the Roman Catholic Church, these reforms are in their infancy, but with the stated aims of music as a form of ministry, there can be little doubt that all these changes are moving towards a position where music, although being an essential part of the liturgy, is nevertheless at its service.

Zambian Anglican Church

To conclude this section on how different traditions use their hymns, we shall consider how hymns are used in the Anglican Church of Zambia. Although Anglican, they are used in a way which is, at first sight, totally different from how the Church of England uses them, though there are similarities in Africa and Asia.

In Zambia, large multi-cultural, multi-lingual urban centres are surrounded by the much smaller township communities. These townships are inhabited predominantly by Africans and the language spoken is the local vernacular. Let us use as an example the northern Copperbelt town of Chingola, where one of the townships is called Kasompe. The small but lively Anglican Church in Kasompe meets in a classroom for a weekly Eucharist. The form of service is similar to the Eucharist which Anglicans in England would attend except that it is in ci-Bemba, the local language. The congregation consists of young children and adults and a vibrant choir drawn from young people in their 'teens and twenties. In the places where hymns are usually sung, the congregation sings hymns, unaccompanied, to tunes similar to those being sung in Great Britain: 'O God, Our Help in Ages Past', 'Love Divine, All Loves Excelling, 'What a Friend We Have in Jesus', and at Christmas time

'Hark! The Herald-angels Sing', 'Silent Night', and 'In the Bleak Mid-winter'. The only difference, again, is that the hymns have been transliterated into ci-Bemba. Often, however, the choir do not join in the singing with the congregation, but wait until the choir 'spot' comes, usually before the service, during communion and after the service. The contrast between what the choir sings and what the congregation sings could not be greater. The choir will usually have written their own hymns or borrowed them from other choirs – the hymns are, like Negro Spirituals, 'popular by origin'. The tunes are traditional melodies which the composer will have heard or been inspired by during a visit to the family 'home' in the rural areas. The hymns are often accompanied by drums and shakers (dried seeds in a bamboo casing) and so lively are the tunes that the choir and frequently the congregation find themselves swaying to the music – this is in contrast to the hymns sung by the congregation when everybody is standing still. What is fascinating are the words of the hymns sung by the choir:

> We shall see Jesus, we shall say according to what we
>   do.
> He will ask how each one worked. Some will say
> 'I was a choir member.'
> What about you, father, sitted there?
> 'You are my God, I was a priest.'
> What about you, mother, sitted there?
> 'I, my Lord, was a Mother's Union Member.'
> To you, father, sitted there?
> 'My Lord, I was a deacon.'
>
> He will come down with his angels to catch his children.
> They have failed to teach, they have come from my house.
> Catch them all and put them in the life prison.
> Everyone will cry 'Why did I become a choir member?'
> 'My God is unfair, I'm put into the life prison.'

1   In heaven there is no sinning.
    Chorus: We shall sing and say hosanna to meet those who
    have gone happy.

We shall sing when reaching heaven, we shall always be happy.

2   And Jesus is the head of that City which is beau
    tiful,
    We shall sing and say hosanna when reaching heaven.
    We shall be happy for ever.[26]

The first example shows how the young people of the choir are being critical of their elders for what they consider to be an abuse of their positions of authority. The choir are warning that such positions will not protect them at the time of God's judgement, so that they should beware. They also remind themselves that being a member of a choir will not protect them from judgement if they have done wrong. The second hymn reveals how heaven is conceptualized as being reunited with those members of tribe or family who have gone before ('who have gone happy'). This is particularly significant for the Zambian living in the towns of the Copperbelt. In pursuit of work they will have been drawn away from their ancestral lands, separated from extended family and forced to live next to people from other tribes. It is little wonder that heaven is seen as being reunited with 'those who have gone happy'.

Another way that Zambian choirs use hymns is to reinforce the message of the preacher. What can be disconcerting for the unsuspecting preacher is that this will happen in the middle of the sermon. If the choir discover that they have a hymn which they think is appropriate, then they will sing it at the point which they consider appropriate – the only hint that the preacher has that they are about to sing is in the tuning up before they begin.

All this reveals how the hymns, although generally accompanying the liturgy in a traditional Anglican way, are also allowing the different groupings within the Church to assert their positions and speak to each other. The singing of the traditional English hymns assert how the Church is heir to the Western missionaries: the newly composed Zambian hymns are not only criticizing the elders, but are also moving on from and even rejecting the Western interpretation of the faith and appealing for a more authentically African interpretation.

Mission Praise: An Ecumenical Hymn Book

The main-line denominations have undertaken major revisions of their hymn books in the 1980s and 1990s. One book which showed that such revisions were essential was *Mission Praise*. Originally compiled for the great evangelistic enterprise 'Mission England', *Mission England Praise* (as it was first known) was found to have an appeal outside of those actively involved in the mission. *Mission Praise* was launched in 1983 and so great was the demand that the publishers found it hard to keep the book constantly in print. The appeal of the book was that it had a selection of traditional hymns alongside contemporary hymns from renewal movements as well as some older Revivalist hymns. So one finds such classics as 'Come, Holy Ghost, Our Souls Inspire', 'Crown Him with Many Crowns', 'Dear Lord and Father of Mankind', 'Abide With Me', contemporary hymns 'Seek Ye First the Kingdom of God', 'Majesty, Worship His Majesty', 'Father, We Adore You', 'He is Lord, He is Risen from the Dead', besides older Revivalist hymns: 'I Need thee Every Hour', 'Blessed Assurance, Jesus is Mine', 'Great is Thy Faithfulness' and 'My Faith Looks Up to Thee'. The book tapped in to an underlying desire for people to go beyond the narrow denominationalism expressed in other Church hymn books. Accordingly *Mission Praise* was (and is) used as a supplement to denominational hymn books and has in some instances replaced them altogether.

Despite its comprehensive nature, *Mission Praise* has a distinctive theological axe to grind which can be seen in the hymns it contains and in the verses it adds to some of the traditional hymns found in its pages. The main features of the book include a large number of hymns addressed exclusively to Jesus:

> Jesus the very thought of thee,
> Jesus my Lord will love me for ever,
> Jesus take me as I am;

a high proportion using the first person singular:

> I am trusting Thee, Lord Jesus,
> I will enter His gates
> Rock of Ages cleft for me;

a low view of humanity:

> He freed me from the servitude of sin
> And now I serve as His slave,

and

> Guilty, vile and helpless we.

There is also a strong theology of glory and a marked sectarian tendency.[27] This combination results in a heavy emphasis on a personal (at the expense of a corporate) relationship with God the Son which issues in total dependence and impotence on the part of the worshipper. This form of dependence, which plays down the fact that human beings were made in the likeness of God, discourages engagement from a world which is regarded in 'Guide Me, O Thou Great Jehovah' as a 'barren land' and encourages fuller engagement in the Christian Community. Such helplessness and impotence before Jesus Christ sets the tone of relationship with authority both inside and outside the Church. All this shows how hymn books, whether 'owned' by a denomination or not, have a theological agenda which have social and political implications.

Hymns in Schools

At the beginning of this book we saw that a considerable number of people (many of whom do not attend Church) encounter hymns through television and radio programmes. For the great number who do not attend Church, the major exposure to hymns is at school assembly. Even in our multi-cultural, multi-faith society every school by law has to have a corporate act of worship where in many instances hymns will be sung. Children spend seven years in primary schools and between five and seven years in secondary schools: a considerable number of hymns, which will have an effect upon the young people, will be sung throughout these years. Not only may they be affected by the hymns themselves, but they will be greatly familiarized with the hymn form, its purposes and function. The minister planning a Church service designed to attract children would be well-advised to discover the hymns that they sing in school and ensure that one or two are included within that service.

Indications are that schools which use hymns choose those which are 'singable', lively and popular and select them according to the themes of the assembly. Some research undertaken among secondary schools in the early 1960s showed the staggering popularity of the hymn book *Songs of Praise*. It was used by 62 per cent of the schools surveyed, compared with 8 per cent which used *Hymns Ancient and Modern* and 2 per cent which used *The BBC Hymn Book*.[28] The hymns which enjoyed 100 per cent (apart from Christmas carols) in the schools were:

All People that on Earth do Dwell
Let Us with a Gladsome Mind
He who would Valiant Be
Praise, My Soul, the King of Heaven
The King of Love my Shepherd is
We Plough the Fields and Scatter.

Hymns sung in 92 per cent of the schools were:

Come, Ye Thankful People, Come
There is a Green Hill Far Away
Dear Lord and Father of Mankind.

Hymns sung in 70 per cent were:

Fight the Good Fight
All Glory, Laud and Honour
When I Survey the Wondrous Cross
Breathe on Me, Breath of God
Now Thank We All Our God
Praise to the Lord, the Almighty
All Creatures of our God and King
Immortal, Invisible, God Only Wise
Jesus Shall Reign.

All of these hymns, popular among children over thirty years ago, continue to be favourites among churchgoers over forty today, thus suggesting the lasting influence of hymns sung at school.

One of the comments that appeared frequently on question-naires was represented by these words:

> Many hymns which are relevant for the Church congregation are alien to a modern pupil, since they contain too many allusions to scriptural images and religious experiences quite beyond his ken.

One of the reasons for the popularity of *Songs of Praise* among schools was probably because it frequently removed Scriptural imagery that was difficult to comprehend. For example, in the last verse of the hymn 'At the Name of Jesus' the imagery of the second coming of Jesus Christ is retained in *Hymns Ancient and Modern*:

> Brothers, this Lord Jesus
> Shall return again,
> With his Father's glory
> With his Angel train,

whereas it is removed in *Songs of Praise*:

> Brothers, this Lord Jesus
> Dwells with us again,
> In his Father's wisdom
> O'er the earth to reign.

However, another reason for the popularity of *Songs of Praise* is the 'musical jewels' to be found in the book.

In a survey published in 1977 the situation in secondary schools had changed dramatically.[29] A typical comment from a secondary school was:

> We seldom sing traditional hymns except Christmas carols. Occasionally 'Kum ba yah' is sung. If music is needed records are played and these are more concerned with world problems, eg 'When I needed a neighbour.'

This comment points towards a shift which is even more marked now than it was in 1977, namely that young people tend to *listen* to rather than *sing* music. Popular music encourages an individualistic response: the volume of the music militates against a communal singing of the lyrics and even dancing can be done alone, even though there are others on the dance floor. In addition, large comprehensive schools face practical difficulties of halls big enough to take large gatherings as well as the reluctance of boys with breaking voices to sing. Add to this serious doubts about the value of worship in a non-religious community and one can see the problems facing school worship. However, in 1977 school worship was very much alive for children of primary school age where the favourites included:

Morning has Broken
All Things Bright and Beautiful
Lord of the Dance
When a Knight Won his Spurs
Kum ba yah
Sing Hosanna
At the Name of Jesus
Glad that I Live am I
Daisies are our Silver
Our Father
The Lord's my Shepherd

Comparing this list of hymns with that from the 1960s research, one is struck immediately by the number of new hymns as well as by the hymns which have little overtly Christian content. Today the situation appears the same except that the number of 'traditional' hymns being sung in schools is far less than it was, creating an even wider gap between schools and churches. I am not aware of any recent research on the hymns sung in schools, but informal soundings in primary schools suggest that there are a number of hymn books in use, one of the most popular being BBC's *Come and Praise*, and a great variety of hymns are being sung. There is a stress on creation and incarnational theology as the hymn-writers struggle to find an understandable language in which faith can be clothed. In 'Peace, Perfect Peace' each of the three verses begins:

> Peace, perfect peace is the gift of Christ our Lord . . .
> Hope, perfect hope, is the gift of Christ our
>   Lord . . .
> Joy, perfect joy, is the gift of Christ our Lord . . .

In 'When a Knight Won his Spurs' Jan Struther (who also wrote 'Lord of All Hopefulness') uses the symbolism of mythical knights and giants to bring alive the message:

> Let faith be my shield and let joy be my steed
> 'gainst the dragons of anger, the ogres of greed.[30]

The search for an appropriate language in which to express the faith and the emphasis on incarnational theology to make the faith alive to the young people's experience are symptomatic of the growing gap between schools and churches, indicating how Christian symbolism is becoming marginal to the experience of so many young people.

Just as different Christian traditions use hymns in a variety of ways, so too hymns are selected in different ways. For some the choirmaster is responsible for the hymns, for others it is the preacher. Those churches which regard hymns as vehicles of doctrine would want to keep their selection in the hands of the preacher. The really brave church allows different people and groupings to make their choice known, as we saw in the Zambian Church where different understandings of faith and different ways in which the congregation expressed their faith were embodied in their hymns. The transliterated hymns of the missionaries, sung by the elders, symbolized the link with the Mother Church in England and in everything except language they were dependent upon the West: in form, in sentiments, in theology and in tune. By contrast, the hymns sung by the choir were very Zambian: they were sung to African tunes, they had an African form, they spoke about their own local community, they reflected their own understanding of God and they specifically rejected those who slavishly followed Western ways. These totally different understandings of the Gospel were given voice in the hymns and were in dialogue with each other in the one act of worship. This was no watering down of expression so that all could agree, but rather the Church was the place where people with very different understandings and viewpoints could worship together and allow the other to express their view. Too often the view of one person or one group of people dominates and no other expression is allowed.

What will have been very apparent from this chapter is the amount of power in the hands of the hymn book editors and compilers. Some denominations such as Methodists, URCs and Baptists appoint groups to produce hymnals under the watchful eye of the parent body, although even here, some of the eyes are less watchful than others. Hymn books produced for Anglicans and Roman Catholics are not regulated in the same way by the churches. The theological interests of different groups are served by small but significant changes in the words of hymns. We saw earlier how hymns can be changed, often in small ways, to suit a different context. We considered how Wesley had changed Issac Watts' 'Our God, Our Help in Ages Past' to 'O God, Our Help in Ages Past'. Looking on a wider scale, compilers of hymn books edit hymns to fit the theological emphases which they are wanting to make. For example, John Wesley omitted the second verse of Charles Wesley's 'Love Divine, All Loves Excelling' because he felt uneasy with the theological concept of achieving perfection in this way. The majority of hymn books have followed John Wesley's omission. However, the second verse has appeared in *Mission Praise* with slight modification to accommodate the book's emphasis on the sinfulness of humanity, its view of the Church as a group very much set apart from the rest of the world, and its emphasis on the work of the Holy Spirit. Notice how Wesley's 'bent to sinning' is changed to the much stronger 'love of sinning':

original version	*Mission Praise 149*
Breathe, O breathe thy loving spirit	Breathe, O breathe Thy loving Spirit
into every troubled breast!	into every troubled breast;
Let us all in thee inherit,	let us all in Thee inherit,
Let us find that second rest.	let us find Thy promised rest;
Take away our bent to sinning,	take away the love of sinning,
Alpha and Omega be;	Alpha and Omega be;
End of faith, as at its beginning.	end of faith, as its beginning,
Set our hearts at liberty.	set out hearts at liberty.

If denominations do not have officially approved hymn books, they tend to use books which were written with that particular denomination in mind: for example, many Anglicans look towards the *Ancient and Modern* and *English Hymnal* family of books while others look towards the *Anglican Hymn Book* (1965) and *Hymns for Today's Church* (1982). With the hymn explosion over the last thirty years there have been a number of books produced for Christians of all denominations and these are being widely used in churches throughout the country. In some instances they are supplementing the denominational hymn books, but in others they are replacing them. The increasing use of such hymn books has pushed the main-line denominations into revising their own hymn books to include some of these new hymns. Again, we can imagine the influence of the editors of these interdenominational books.

Another example of the power of editors and compilers reveals how an opportunity to make an ecumenical statement has been missed. One of the outcomes of the recent revisions of the hymn books of the main-line denominations is that some well-known hymns are provided with different words in each book. This is regrettable in that the singing of common hymns was one thing that all Christians, regardless of denominational background, could do together; it is also paradoxical that in a period of greater ecumenical sharing the singing of hymns could be potentially divisive. The URC had originally hoped to co-operate with the Methodists to produce an ecumenical hymn book, but, sadly, this did not happen. Each denomination will have had sound theological reasons for the alterations, but the differences present a sad testimony. An example of this can be seen in last verse of 'Immortal, Invisible, God Only Wise'; where the Methodist *Hymns and Psalms* produces the original:

> Great Father of glory, pure Father of light.
> Thine angels adore thee, all veiling their sight;
> All laud we would render, O help us to see
> 'Tis only the splendour of light hideth thee,

the URC's *Rejoice and Sing* reads:

Great Father of glory: O help us to see
'tis only the splendour of light hideth thee.
And so let thy glory, Almighty, impart,
through Christ in the story, thy Christ to the heart.

Finally, *Baptist Praise and Worship* reads:

Great Father of glory, pure Father of light,
thine angels adore thee, all veiling their sight;
but of all thy rich graces this grace, Lord impart:
take the veil from our faces, the veil from our heart.

All praise we would render: O help us to see,
'tis only the splendour of light hideth thee;
and so let thy glory, Almighty, impart,
through Christ in the story, thy Christ to the heart.

7

Hymns Without Worship

One of the advantages of pure congregational singing is that you can join in the singing whether you have a voice or not. The disadvantage is that your neighbours can do the same.

Charles Dudley Warner

The usual, though by no means the only, place for singing hymns is in Church and within worship. We have seen how people sang hymns in Church, though presumably not always within the liturgy, in order to keep their spirits when their Bishop Ambrose was under threat from the Empress Justina. In the same chapter we saw how people adapted carols and sang them outside Church because they were not given a voice inside. We have also seen how people sang hymns on their Whit walks, at football and rugby matches and at the Proms. People sing hymns on pilgrimages and on processions. Hymns evoke spirituality and nostalgia and can draw a sense of the presence of God into situations. Hymns provide a 'spiritual building' in which people can feel at home and at ease. In many of these instances, hymns have been used almost spontaneously in that the yearning (both conscious and sub-conscious) to link God with particular events or moments has caused the singing of hymns. It is one of the main contentions of this book that the wealth and creativity found within hymns can be harnessed and drawn upon even more, though there will be consequences for our ecclesiology. In this chapter there are examples of how hymns can be used in discussion groups of various kinds.

Too often the Church discussion group has a subject and agenda set by the cleric leading the group or by lay people who have a grasp of traditional theological language. So often discussions are cerebral, using dialogue and terms which will be familiar to some, but by no means to all, of the group. Hymns provide a way that enables many to have an input into the agenda and the discussion because all people can suggest hymns which will reflect their theological preferences. If the hymns are sung as well as discussed, then not only are all the members of the group given a voice but the group encounter is able to extend beyond a mere cerebral level. Here are some examples based upon groups and discussions in which I have been involved. Details from the discussion are mixed with comments on the method employed.

One study group agreed to meet for five sessions to discuss hymns. This particular group had a wide cross-section of theological view-points and knowledge of Scripture; it had an average of twelve regular members, some of whom were new to the group. Ages ranged from the mid-thirties to the mid-eighties and although all worshipped regularly at an Anglican church, some were from Baptist and Brethren backgrounds. Each member was asked to bring a hymn which spoke powerfully about their faith, though the hour-and-a-half set aside only allowed two or maybe three hymns to be discussed. One hymn that was selected was 'How Great Thou Art'. First of all the hymn was sung by everybody – the importance of singing the hymn before discussing it is that the person selecting it is returned to the experience with which the hymn is associated. The person was then asked why that particular hymn had been chosen: this provides an opportunity for them to speak about a significant occasion in his or her life. The amount of detail revealed will depend upon the size of the group and how confident the person is in sharing what often proves to have been a formative and intensely personal experience. This in itself prompts exploration and discussion. The leader then asked the group what the hymn said about God and humanity whereupon discussion centred on the contrast between the great creator God as shown in the words:

> O Lord my God, when I in awesome wonder,
> Consider all the works Thy hand hath made . . .

and the sinfulness of humanity:

> That on the cross, my burden gladly bearing,
> He bled and died to take away my sin.

Although some felt that it was justified to have this great contrast in order to enhance God's greatness, others felt that the high view of God, combined with a low view of humanity and a strong view of sin which emphasized God's saving work through Jesus Christ, implied a threat to those who do not follow Christ. There then emerged an animated debate on the whole question of the judgement which the hymn implied would fall upon those who were not followers of Christ. Some noted the reference to 'home' in the verse:

> When Christ shall come with shout of acclamation,
> To take me home, what joy shall fill my heart . . .

It was agreed that 'home' meant being with God, which raised questions about our relationship with this world. If our real home was not in this world, how seriously should the world and its problems be taken? How far should we try to change the world in order to make it a reflection of God's Kingdom and how far should this world be endured because it was of little consequence in comparison to the world to come? The discussion then moved on to the Lord's Prayer to discover whether the references to the Kingdom found there ('Thy Kingdom come, Thy will be done on earth as it is in heaven') could shed any light on the question of whether there should be any real investment in this life and in this world. As the debate continued it became apparent that some considered it to be the task of Christians to establish God's Kingdom here, whereas others felt that this world was beyond saving and would in time be destroyed and replaced by a new and perfect creation. It was pointed out that both these views could be extrapolated from Scripture.

Another question which arose from the hymn was whether salvation could only come through Christ. There were discussions about whether the faithful of other religions could be brought to God or whether it was only through Christ as the hymn asserts. The group was strongly divided on this, but there was ample opportunity to explore the very significant question of how Christians relate to other faiths. If there had been more time, the group could have been told the story behind the hymn which would have led on to further exploration of how God views creation in the Scriptures. The hymn is the work of the British missionary and evangelist Stuart Hine who was born in 1899. The hymn came into English via Swedish and Russian. The original poem was written (in Swedish) by Carl Boberg who was an evangelist, Member of Parliament and a journalist. Boberg was converted to Evangelical Christianity in his 'teens and went to Bible College. He was moved to write his poem one summer's evening as he stood looking across the Monsteras inlet at a rainbow that had formed following a storm and listening to a distant church bell. Boberg's hymn was published in several Swedish hymn books, but it was a Russian version which Stuart Hine heard in the western Ukraine where he was a missionary in the 1920s. Hine wrote the first three verses while engaged in evangelistic work in the Carpathian mountains on the borders of Russia and Romania and the fourth verse on his return to Britain in 1948. At that time thousands of refugees from Russia and other parts of Eastern Europe came to England with the question in their minds about when they would be able to return home. In an essay about the hymn Hine wrote:

> What better message for the homeless than that the One who went to prepare a place for the 'displaced', of the God who invites into his own home those who will come to him through Christ.[1]

The verse to which Hine was referring (with its reference to 'home') has already been quoted.

Another way in which the hymn could have been the source of a fruitful discussion would have been to explore how the creation story was used in Genesis 1 as a source of encouragement to another group of 'refugees' – the dispirited Israelites who had been forced out of their beloved land and set in exile in Babylon. How does this compare to the way in which Hine has used it in his hymn?

Moving on to other discussions at other times, a clergyman brought the hymn 'To God be the Glory'. After it had been sung, the clergyman spoke movingly about how he came to

know and value this hymn when he had attended a Baptist
church in the years of his national service. It became a favourite
during the early Billy Graham Crusades which provided a
further boost to his faith and challenge to service. The clergyman was appointed rector of a parish in Somerset which had
within it an old 'mission church'. He was pleased to discover
that the hymn was part of the hymn tradition of this church.
There was a need to replace the old mission church, which so
many had come to love, with a new building. There were
problems over how the new building could be financed, but the
congregation's faith and commitment bore fruit:

> Great things He hath taught us, great things He hath done,
> And great our rejoicing through Jesus the Son;
> But purer, and higher, and greater will be
> Our wonder, our transport, when Jesus we see.

The hymn became an expression of the congregation's reali-
zation of the goodness, grace and love of God towards them.
Many people, not least the oldest members, including one
baptized in the mission church in 1898, were overwhelmed and
humbled by having a share in something they always thought
would remain a dream. They had a sense of unworthiness:

> O perfect redemption, the purchase of blood,
> To every believer – the promise of God;
> The vilest offender who truly believes,
> That moment from Jesus a pardon receives.

The hymn was part of the final worship in the old mission
church in 1989, it was sung in the shell of the new building as
it was being built and it was a key feature in the first services in
the completed church and at its dedication service in November
1990. When the foundation stone for the new church was laid
in March 1990 it was natural for the inscription on the stone
not to say 'To the Glory of God' as it says on so many such
stones, but 'To God be the Glory'.

The group was then told the story of the hymn and hymn-
writer. It was written by Frances Jane van Alstyne (1820–1915)
who is better known as Fanny Crosby. She was born in New
York and was totally blind from infancy – a fact which adds

particular poignancy to the final verse (quoted in full above) which concludes the hymn with the words:

> But purer, and higher, and greater will be
> Our wonder, our transport, when Jesus we *see*.

Fanny Crosby was converted to Evangelical religion during the singing of Isaac Watt's hymn 'Here, Lord, I Give Myself Away'. Later she met Ira Sankey who wrote the music to many of her hymns. She was a prolific writer producing more than 8,000 hymns. Many of her hymns point to the great things that God has done, rather than telling men and women how to behave. The above hymn was written in the early 1870s and was used by Sankey in his British crusade in 1873 but then lapsed into obscurity until it was revived by the Billy Graham evangelistic organization in the 1950s and used in the London Crusade in 1954. It was immediately popular with those who attended the crusades at Harringay Stadium and became the theme hymn for the crusade.

The group went on to discuss the hymn's view of God and humanity, noting that God was a great and loving father, but human beings could be 'vile' and only be given life through Jesus:

> O come to the Father through Jesus the Son.

This led to discussion on the relationship between God and his creation as well as to how people understood atonement:

> Who yielded his Life an atonement for sin,
> And opened the Life gate that all may go in.

As well as using hymns in this somewhat general way in discussion groups, it is also possible to use them in more specific ways, to develop a particular theological theme. For example, if 'heaven' was the theme, people could be encouraged to bring along hymns that speak on this subject. There was such a discussion when the hymn 'Jerusalem the Golden' was used. This hymn was part of a long Latin poem (some 3,000 lines) entitled 'De contemptu mundi' ('On Contempt of the World') written by Bernard of Murles around 1140 when he was a monk at the great Benedictine Abbey in Cluny, France.

Other hymns that have been translated from the same poem
are 'Brief Life is Here our Portion', 'The World is Very Evil'
and 'For Thee, O Dear, Dear Country'.

At first 'Jerusalem the Golden' produced little response until
the group leader explained the significance of Jerusalem in
Jewish history, beginning with the founding of the city, continuing with its use in Isaiah and the psalms and how Jerusalem
came to be associated with heaven. The hymn was printed in
Hymns Ancient and Modern with a quote from Revelation 21.18,
'And the city was pure gold', which gave the opportunity to
consider the view of heaven in the Book of Revelation. The
discussion felt that heaven only became a real question when
one is under pressure of some kind. One group member, who
prayed regularly for political prisoners in USSR, spoke of one
who had been imprisoned for forty-seven years and was sustained by a 'picture' of heaven. The discussion moved on to
how the Book of Revelation was probably written to sustain
those under a similar kind of political pressure. This particular
hymn (set in a poem expressing contempt of the world) discouraged its singers from putting any kind of investment in this
world but to look towards the next. The aspirations of the
twelfth-century monk were encouraged upon nineteenth-
century England. The hymn describes heaven (Jerusalem the
golden) as 'serene', 'the pastures of the blessed', a place of
'care released', a place where there is 'triumph' and 'feast'. It
is a 'sweet and blessed country', 'home of God's elect' and a
'dear land of rest'. Where heaven was described as 'the home
of God's elect' did this mean that people would encounter their
departed loved ones?

Such a view of heaven can be contrasted with another to be
found in the hymn (again brought forward at a discussion
group) 'O Holy City, Seen of John'. This was written by W.
Russell Bowie (1882–1969) and while inspired by St John's
vision in Revelation 21 and using the imagery of that book,
nevertheless earths the vision in this world in terms of 'brotherhood' and 'human good', bewailing Christians who rest
content with lust, greed and extortion. The final verse concludes:

> lo, how its splendour challenges
> the souls that greatly dare:
> yea, bids us seize the whole of life
> and build its glory there.

The two visions of heaven based on the same chapter of the same book of the Bible provide a stimulating discussion on how the same imagery can be differently interpreted and understood. One can explore how different social and cultural circumstances evoke different reactions. Bowie had greater confidence in the ability to change twentieth-century society than the translator did in the nineteenth. This leads on to exploring different images of heaven (for instance, as places of wealth, reunion with loved ones, of being with God) and discovering one which is helpful for contemporary society.

It is also possible to use hymns for adult confirmation classes. There will be a number of topics which the leader of the classes will want to cover, but if hymns are used at some point it will again enable people to bring their own theological concerns forward. One person brought the hymn 'Lord of All Hopefulness'. He found this hymn a great comfort because it prayed for God's continuing presence at the break of day, at noon, evening and the end of the day. The discussion centred around the whole question of God's presence, on the one hand noting how it could be a great support, and people gave examples from their lives of where they felt God's support and presence, but, on the other hand, noting how it could also be judgemental. This latter point was brought out after a discussion of verses from Psalm 139:

> Where could I go to escape your spirit?
> Where could I flee from your presence?
> If I climb the heavens, you are there,
> there too, if I lie in Sheol.
>
> If I flew to the point of sunrise,
> or westward across the sea,
> your hand would still be guiding me,
> your right hand holding me.

Some felt that these verses revealed the psalmist trying to escape God's presence, whereas others saw them as a positive assertion of God's omnipresence. Both these positions were explored from biblical and contemporary perspectives.

The person requesting this hymn also identified with the line in the second verse –

Whose strong hands were skilled at the plane and the lathe

– because he enjoyed woodwork and found it a time of relaxation and reflection. This led to a fruitful discussion about the person and identity of Jesus Christ.

There are occasions when discussions link the music of hymns to their words. One such occasion happened with 'Lord Jesus Christ'. This hymn was written in the late 1950s when the author, Patrick Appleford, was parish priest in Poplar, East London. The repetition of 'Mary's Son' and its being set alongside 'Son of God' shows the hymn's purpose of teaching who Jesus Christ was and encouraging singers to identify with him. The repetition of the phrase 'into our lives your power breaks through' and the ending of each verse with 'living Lord' mark out the hymn-writer's intention of showing that Christ was not simply a figure of the past but is still alive, vibrant and powerful today. One member wondered why each verse ended with a declining melody (B, C#, D) to the words 'living Lord' rather than an ascending melody which would emphasize the triumph of the Living Lord. After discussion it was felt that the ordinary, unexciting ending somehow related the message it was trying to transmit to ordinary people who do not have a great deal of excitement in their lives; the music perfectly fitted the sentiments of the words which was why the hymn was so powerful.

Another hymn that has frequently been requested in groups is Robert Bridges' 'All My Hope on God is Founded'. People have spoken movingly of this hymn reflecting how they felt sustained by God's love in times of great difficulty. Others have spoken of how their pride has been challenged with the words:

Pride of man and earthly glory,
sword and crown betray his trust;

what with care and toil he buildeth,
tower and temple, fall to dust.

There have been debates about how Bridges (who was poet laureate) was encouraging people to put their trust in God rather than in the trappings of power and authority which appeared so transitory. This hymn is well known and is a good example of how the right music has freed it to become so popular. The hymn as we have it is loosely based on a German hymn by Joachim Neander (1650–80), a Christian pastor. I Timothy 6.17 which warns the rich that they are not to look down on other people and that they are not

to set their hopes on money, which is untrustworthy, but on God who, out of his riches, gives us all that we need for our happiness

is the passage upon which the hymn is composed. When Bridges published the hymn in his 1899 *Yattendon Hymnal* it was set to the tune to which Neander had originally written it. However, it began to gain its real popularity after being set to Herbert Howells' lively tune 'Michael'. Howells had been contacted by the director of music at Charterhouse School and asked to compose a new tune to the hymn. Howells wrote the tune immediately upon receiving it, at the very breakfast table where he had opened the letter containing the request. Howells called it 'Michael' after his son who had died in infancy. One discussion on this story conjectured that behind Bridges' poetry lies an experience of deep pain in which the poet found comfort and support in God. Howells had also experienced something similar and, detecting this behind Bridges' hymn, was able to match the experience expressed through poetry with a similar experience expressed through music.

In one discussion of this hymn, the version used was taken from *Hymns for Today's Church* which has been modified from the original version found in *Hymns Ancient and Modern*. The consequent discussion was centred around the varying theological emphases in the different versions, thereby revealing another way in which hymns can provide springboards for debate. First, the creative power and might of God which are addressed in verse 3 of the original are omitted in *Hymns for Today's Church*:

> God's great goodness aye endureth,
> Deep his wisdom, passing thought:
> Splendour, light and life attend him,
> Beauty springeth out of naught.
> Evermore
> From his store
> New-born worlds rise and adore.

The fourth verse (now the third in the later version) undergoes a radical shift which focuses attention from this world on to the next:

Hymns Ancient and Modern	*Hymns for Today's Church*
Daily doth th'Almighty Giver	Day by day our mighty giver
Bounteous gifts on us bestow;	grant to us his gifts of love
His desire our soul delighteth,	in his will our souls find
Pleasure leads us where we go.	pleasure,
Love doth stand	leading to our home above:
At his hand;	Love shall stand
Joy doth wait on his command.	at his hand,
	joy shall wait for his command

The result of this shift, together with the omission of the third verse which stresses how God's locus of activity is in this world, is that this world is devalued (especially with the reference to 'our home above') and any encouragement to reform the unjust structures within this world is lost.

A final example shows that disagreement over whether a hymn should be sung can bring creative encounters. Fred Kaan's hymn 'Sing We a Song of High Revolt', based on the Magnificat, caused strong disagreements within one group, some definitely liking it, others very much the opposite. The lines which caused the greatest reaction were:

> He calls us to revolt and fight
> With him for what is just and right.

Some argued that Christ had already done this at Calvary, but some felt that although the 'war' had been won at Calvary, some battles were still being fought, though in the knowledge that the war had been won. Some were attracted to the hymn because it encouraged action, one person commenting, 'It makes me feel that I should get off my butt and do something'; others felt that it did not leave God any space to do the work. There was a debate about how God works through human beings, but that human beings had the problem of discerning God's will. A number of people objected to the word 'revolt' because it implied a violence which they believed went contrary to the Christian Gospel. It would not be an attractive hymn to singers who identified themselves with the rich:

> The rich are left with empty hands.

Though the poor would look upon the hymn favourably

> He satisfies with bread and cup
> The hungry men of many lands

The group then studied St Luke's version of the Magnificat (Luke 1. 46–55) and compared it with the hymn, noting that Scripture, like the hymn, was written from a particular social and cultural perspective and that it was certainly not politically neutral. The group were reminded that Fred Kaan had spent a number of years working for the World Council of Churches in Geneva at a time when it had a high political profile and the preferential option for the poor, which figures in Kaan's hymns, figured highly in the World Council's radical theological approach. The group then sang Timothy Dudley Smith's version of the Magnificat: 'Tell Out, My Soul, the Greatness of the Lord'. A number within the group felt more at home with the less political stance of this hymn and noted that it stressed the praise of God, whereas Kaan's hymn stressed human endeavour. It was noted, once again, how people interpret passages of Scripture and Christian symbols from their own perspective and that theology can never be neutral or apolitical. There then followed a discussion as to how one would react to a hymn with which one disagreed. All agreed that they would not sing it, though if there was a group of people who showed strong preferences for the hymn those who disliked it would be willing for it to be sung. None indicated that this would prevent them from returning to the Church.

Without exception, all the people in groups encouraged to use hymns as bases for discussion found this method helpful and challenging. Some, who have a high view of Scripture, find it difficult to be critical of Scriptural texts, whereas our group members had no such restraints when discussing hymns. Others who feel overwhelmed by the knowledge of Scripture that some people have, feel confident to take a fuller part when hymns are the basis of discussion. Others felt that hymns provided a more relaxed method of discussing, especially as the sessions included singing. The value of singing the hymn to be examined was in putting people in touch experientially with the text. Using hymns also encouraged those who did not feel confident or knowledgeable of the Bible to make substantial contributions to the discussion.

A great number of hymns (and this is especially true of older hymns) tend to be based on specific biblical passages; some hymn books helpfully provide the Bible reference. Using hymns as a basis for discussion helps a group move with ease and naturalness between contemporary experience to the Bible to doctrine and to prayer, thereby giving people a number of entry points into the discussion. To put this more theologically, by being freed to select their own hymns participants were able to express their theology in a form and concept which spoke to them. Some communicated more naturally using liturgical theology as they sang the hymns, others by narrative theology as they brought alive what the hymn meant by telling how it related to their lives, yet others by propositional theology as they explored the doctrines to which the hymns referred. What was of great significance was that many people acknowledged the value of different ways of communicating theologically without saying that one way was better or superior to another.

The hymns selected have tended to identify sub-groups. For example, some hymns are favourites of the politically radical, some of Catholics, some of Charismatics and some of those who are Calvinist in their theology. This reinforces earlier observations of hymns reflecting theological and cultural backgrounds. A key person in this exercise is the group leader who needs to be 'bilingual' in the sense that she or he needs to know the Scripture and traditions as well as the background and culture in which the group is operating.

One great asset in using hymns as a means of discussion is that they allow disagreement within a context of unity. Standing or sitting together, singing the same words at the same time all create an atmosphere of unity. Even though people may interpret a hymn differently, singing it together provides a strong common bond: such unity provides an important witness. Dr Elizabeth Templeton, who attended the 1988 Lambeth Conference of Anglican Bishops as a theological consultant, comments upon this kind of unity in the context of another debate:

> The world is used to unity of all sorts, to the unity of solidarity in campaigns, unity in resistance, communities of party, creed, interest. But it is not used to such unity as this: that, for example, those who find the exclusion of women from the priesthood an intolerable apartheid and those who find the inclusion a violation of God's will should enter upon another's suffering. Somewhere in there, authority lies.[2]

This concept of unity indicates that the need for togetherness is greater than the need for agreement, pointing towards a far deeper bond of unity than may be apparent and allowing different interpretations of common texts and symbols. The stronger the bond between a group, the greater the range of disagreement that will be permitted.

In conclusion, here is a list of questions that may be helpful in approaching the discussion of hymns. It needs to be stressed that it is not always possible to find answers to all the questions, nor will all the questions be relevant on all occasions, but they serve as a guide:

1 Why is it important to the person who has selected it?
2 By whom was the hymn written?
3 Under what circumstances was it written: what is the story behind it?
4 For what occasion and place was it written?
5 Where is it usually sung (at weddings, funerals, Holy

Communion), was it meant to be sung there and by whom was it meant to be sung?

6   What is the theological, social, cultural, historical background?

7   Has the hymn been altered at all? If so, why?

8   What does it say about God, humanity and salvation?

9   What function do hymns play in the tradition from which it has come? Do they normally accompany the liturgy or preach the doctrine, or what?

10 What can be discovered about the tune? Was it written for this particular hymn? Does it express through music what the words are trying to express? What were the circumstances under which it was written?

8

Sing a New Song to the Lord

*If an ignorant shepherdess can be raised to mystical wisdom, it is
true she is ignorant of metaphysics and theology, not that she is an
ignorant; she has faith, and by faith she grasps in their divine
source those truths which theologians disclose in the sweat of their
brows.*

Jacques Maritain

We have seen how hymns can be treasure-houses giving a voice
to those who have great faith and much theology to express.
Hymns not only communicate the content of the theology in
ways that people can grasp, but they also communicate through
a medium (that is, of singing) with which people can feel at
ease. Those not professionally trained in theology may feel
intimidated and possibly dis-abled in trying to express theological truths using the language of the academic theologian, but
the same people would probably feel much more at ease
expressing these same truths through hymns. Hymns also allow
the articulation of controversial opinions which not all the congregation would hold: the singing of hymns encourages a standing together in solidarity and an acceptance of people whose
opinions not everybody in the congregation would share.

There is undoubtedly greater lay involvement in churches
than there has ever been. Certainly the Anglican Church has
full lay representation on her major decision-making bodies
and the lay voice is well represented within the local church.
However, the decision-making processes within the Church are
predominantly middle-class designed and middle-class admin-
istered. The Church may no longer be solely dominated by the
clergy in the way that it was, but power is now concentrated in

the hands of a middle-class laity and clergy. There is still an elitism within the Church, but its character has changed.

Just as the decision-making bodies of the Church only provide access to the corridors of power for the few, so too in its articulation of faith, the Church acknowledges means of expression which are only accessible to a few. In a fascinating piece of research published under the title *Everyday Men – Living in a Climate of Unbelief*, Dr Roger Edrington, a Churches of Christ minister, interviewed fifty working-class men in Birmingham who had no links at all with Church even though the majority of them professed a belief in God. Through open and patient listening, Edrington discovered that many of them prayed regularly though they prayed in private because they felt embarrassed about it and they thought that their way of praying did not fit with the conventional way advocated by the churches. Edrington also discovered that they had their own understandings of Jesus Christ. One man, for instance, remembered an incident in the army when he saw an officer risk his life in the middle of a fire fight to rescue a wounded soldier. The officer carried the soldier on his back to safety. The man whom Edrington was interviewing explained Christ in terms of the officer rescuing the soldier under fire, but he had not shared this image with anybody else because it did not fit with conventional Christian understandings. Traditional language and imagery of the Church did not speak to the experience of those whom Edrington interviewed and they were reluctant to share this with others for fear of being ridiculed. In this sense, the position of the many whose voice and forms of expression are not heard is no different from the people in the medieval times who had to adapt carols in order to be able to praise God.

Unfortunately, this elitism in theological expression in churches is also found in musical expression. In so many places, the choice of the hymns is left to one or two people who impose their musical – and therefore their theological – preferences upon the majority. Hymns provide the channel through which people can offer themselves to God; if this channel is blocked as hymns are rejected, then people will feel that they have been rejected and turn elsewhere (or nowhere) to find this fulfilment. Walter Hollenweger writes:

what is good music, also good church music, is decided by those who have privilege and power in church and society. Their taste and their judgement can only be challenged by their peers and not by musical outsiders, even if these outsiders are the overwhelming majority of the population.

Hollenweger goes on to point out the outcome of this narrowness:

> The number of people following these opinion-makers in church music is very small indeed, a tiny minority in society at large. But since the majority is considered incompetent, the only thing left to the majority, which has no power in these matters, is to demonstrate their disappointment or probably their 'couldn't-care-less' attitude. So they absent themselves from our music and our liturgies.[1]

What would be the implications for the Church of allowing people in the pew a greater say in the hymns, and therefore the theology, of the Church? It may well be possible for churches to devise a system in which the congregation as a whole would have a greater opportunity to join in the selection of hymns. First, when people realized that the Church had accepted and acknowledged their understanding of their relationship with God as expressed through the hymn, they would feel more positive towards an organization which was clearly attempting to listen to what they were wanting to say. This would encourage a loyalty and commitment towards the Church. This loyalty and commitment, in turn, would lead to a desire to express opinions and ideas about the running and governing of the organization. After all, if a person's voice was being heard, acknowledged and accepted within the worship, then this same person would grow in sufficient self-confidence to want to have their voice acknowledged and accepted outside the worship and in the places where decisions are made.

Secondly, worship would contain a variety of styles of music which would reflect some of the breadth of God's creation. Why should Graham Kendrick's 'Shine, Jesus, Shine' not be sung in the same service as Lyte's 'Praise, My Soul, the King of Heaven'? Why should Fred Kaan's 'Let Us Talents and

Tongues Employ', which is set to Doreen Potter's arrangement of the Jamaican folksong 'Linstead Market', not be sung in the same service as Pott's 'Angel Voices Ever Singing'? Provided the hymns express the heartfelt faith and aspirations of members of the community, then such variety will enrich the people's offering to God in worship. It is frequently the case that while the person responsible for selecting the hymns in a service may be concerned about a consistency in musical style, members of the congregation often appreciate variety. Just as adults listen particularly intently to sermons directed towards children, so too they enjoy singing children's songs which both provide a refreshing change from the style of hymns they sing at other times and remind them of an earlier stage of their Christian journey. This different way of selecting need not lead to a jumbled collection of hymns where there is no rationale for choice (there may be a liturgical theme around which the service is planned) but there is no reason why the hymns should not come from a variety of traditions. In a small way this already happens at worship where a choir has a high profile: the choir will select music from the Church's great choral tradition and offer this as their worship to God while the congregation will offer their worship through hymns.

Thirdly, one of the greatest temptations before all churches is that they become bastions protecting their members from God's world instead of platforms liberating their members to enter more deeply into God's world. Appropriately chosen hymns can affirm this 'ark' mentality, encouraging worshippers to rest in God's activities of the past without turning their attention to God's activity in the present and the future. In a book on the nineteenth-century Danish hymn-writer Grundtvig, Christian Thodberg writes:

> As long as our hymns fail to express the living feeling that we have already passed over from death into life, that we have found the everlasting life in God's love and have drunk from the chalice of His salvation, but express only the memory of God's great and wonderful works among the children of man and the hope of redemption from the chains of vanity, then they remain flat and weak compared with what the song of

God's servant Moses, and the psalms of David and Asaph meant to Israel's people who believed.[2]

If people are enabled to select hymns from their varied backgrounds then there is a strong likelihood that there will be vigorous dialogue both inside and outside worship which should discourage the music as a whole from being 'flat and weak'. On the contrary, the dialogue between different theological approaches which will be conducted through the hymns in worship will be reflecting the dialogue which will be happening outside the Church. Furthermore, the Church becomes a place where people will recognize that the really important matters of life and death are taken seriously and debated in a number of different arenas.

Fourthly, there can be no doubt that by giving a wider cross-section of churchgoers a voice in the worship and, consequently, in the decision-making processes of the Church, the character of the Church will be affected: it will be able to reflect, represent and express the richness of God's creation. However, the method suggested here does not *remove* the voice of those who are leaders within the Church, but it does suggest that some kind of reassessment is required. In the Anglican Church the ordained ministry (bishops, priests and deacons) is distinct from, though it cannot make sense apart from, the ministry of the whole people of God, the Church. The Anglican understanding of the relationship between these two ministries is expressed in the service of the ordination of priests:

> We praise and glorify you [Almighty Father] that by his death he has overcome death; and that, having ascended into heaven, he has given his gifts abundantly, making some, apostles; some, prophets; some, evangelists; some, pastors and teachers; to equip your people for the work of ministry and to build up his body.
>
> And now we give you thanks that you have called these your servants, whom we ordain in your name, to share this ministry entrusted to your Church.[3]

An article in *The Study of Anglicanism* sums the position up:

> The revised Anglican ordinals generally emphasize that the exist-

ence and exercise of ordained ministry cannot be divorced from
the corporate ministry of the community . . . Nevertheless, Anglicanism continues to resist pragmatic accounts of ordination as
community delegation. The Anglican-Reformed dialogue report
'God's Reign and Our Unity' (London, 1984), for example,
argues that 'priests' exercise 'their priestly office' neither apart
from the priesthood of the whole body, nor by derivation from
the priesthood of the whole body; and 'Ministry and Ordination'
in the ARCIC 'Final Report' proposes that ordained ministry 'is
not an extension of the common Christian priesthood but
belongs to another realm of the gifts of the Spirit'.[4]

This relationship between priest and people is reflected in
Church life by the way both need to agree how things are to
be done (especially with regard to worship). The priest is also
bound by an oath of obedience to the bishop of the diocese
which will link him or her with the universal Church of Christ.
Thus, if the priest wishes to change an established pattern of
services, he or she could not do so without agreement of the
people; similarly, if the congregation wish to make changes,
this cannot happen without agreement of the priest.

To return to the question of hymns, if the balance of Church
polity is to be retained, the priest would still have the opportunity to select hymns. But the emphasis should be on the
priest being able to make his or her selection rather than altering
or refusing those which various groups within the congregation
would want. By the leader of the worship retaining the right to
select some of the hymns, new themes and new insights could
be introduced and some kind of balance retained. So, if the
priest (or leader of the worship) wanted to highlight the plight
of the oppressed, the South African hymn, 'We are Marching
in the Light of God' may, for example, be introduced. If there
was a celebration of a Celtic saint, one of the Celtic hymns 'I
Bind unto Myself Today' (St Patrick's Breastplate) or 'Lord of
All Hopefulness' could be used. A sermon on the call and song
of Mary (Luke 1) might be illustrated with Fred Kaan's 'Sing
We a Song of High Revolt'; the Taizé chant 'How Blest are
Those who are Poor' could be used to extend the theme of a
talk on the Sermon on the Mount (Matthew 5). Hymns provide

the leader of worship with the opportunity to highlight and expound upon a theme through a medium which is alternative to and often more powerful than words. If there were a genuine dialogue between priest and people in the construction of the liturgy, it would be a reflection of a wider relationship in which the Church community would be able to live with differences of opinion and theology rather than ignoring or silencing those voices that the majority do not wish to hear. Belonging to such a community would not always be comfortable, but an important message about the nature of unity would be conveyed.

Taking hymns seriously in the way proposed in this book will also raise questions about appropriate models of doing theology. In the last twenty years, Liberation Theology has criticized how Western academic theology has given the impression that the Western way is the only way of doing theology. Desmond Tutu in an address on 'The Theology of Liberation' said:

> But we note that some of the best theologies have come not from the undisturbed peace of a don's study, or his speculations in a university seminar, but from a situation where they have been hammered out on the anvil of adversity, in the heat of the battle, or soon thereafter. For too long Western theology has wanted to lay claim to a university that it cannot too easily call its own. Christians have found that the answers they possessed were answers to questions that nobody in different situations was asking. New theologies have arisen, addressing themselves to the issues in front of them. Consequently we have in our midst now the theology of Liberation, as developed in Latin America, and Black Theology, developed in the USA and Southern Africa.[5]

Tutu gave this address in 1978 when he and his country were suffering under the iron grip of apartheid. Although Tutu was steeped in the Western theological tradition, he clearly did not feel that, by itself, it gave much support in the situation in which he found himself. This has been the experience of many others who have been struggling to make sense of their Christian faith in the light of their own local cultural and political contexts. Applying Western models of theology which have evolved in Western contexts has dis-abled people in non-Western countries trying to make sense of what was happening in the light of their Christian faith. Consequently, churches were faced with the dilemma that they either found more appropriate ways of communicating theology or they would find themselves relegated to the realm of the irrelevant or they would be empty. Different cultures communicate in different ways. For example, in the revival of the Pentecostal Churches in the early 1900s, the Black churches developed an oral liturgy and a narrative theology. They used dreams and visions as a form of iconography in their communities and expressed their understanding of the relationship between mind and body in their praying for the sick. At the time, this was considered an inferior form of theology, but more and more it is being accepted not as inferior but simply different. As one third world theologian commented, Western academic theology should not confuse scholarship with the defence of its cultural prejudices.[6]

Western theologies have made a huge contribution towards the understanding and interpretation of God's activity in the world: the length and development of their traditions continue to provide a unique tool of interpretation. But Western theologies need to be set in dialogue with other ways of doing theology, so that the Universal Church can be enriched. Moreover, Western theologies have been under the control of a group drawn from a relatively small cross-section of society. Just as there is a need to have a dialogue between theology in the West and theologies done elsewhere in the world, so too there is a need to have a dialogue between theology as controlled by the small cross-section of British society and those (like the men whom Edrington interviewed) whose voices have not been heard. The popularity of hymns among those who rarely, if ever, darken the doors of our churches indicate that such a dialogue, which is long overdue, is possible.

Mission

There are three major issues, all closely related, which hymns raise about mission. First, as we have seen there are many people, both inside and outside the Church, who have a faith which needs to be recognized and acknowledged. Second, if we are to acknowledge the faith of others, there is a need for real listening. But real listening is not sitting with one's comments and reponses already formulated, but listening without having made evaluative judgements before the person – or the song – is finished. The risk of listening is that the listener may be changed. Psychotherapist Carl Rogers writes about this risk of being changed, which is, of course, at the heart of the Christian Gospel:

> If you really understand another person in this way, if you are willing to enter his private world and see the way life appears to him, without any attempts to make evaluative judgements, you run the risk of being changed yourself. You might see it his way, you might find yourself influenced in your attitudes or your personality. This risk of being changed is one of the most frightening prospects most of us can face. If I enter, as fully as I am able, into the private world of a neurotic or psychotic individual, isn't there a risk that I might become lost in that world? . . . The great majority of us could not 'listen'; we would find ourselves compelled to 'evaluate', because listening would seem too dangerous. So the first requirement is courage, and we do not always have it.[7]

There are a number of theologians who take great pains to listen to those whose views are not usually heard: to the disabled, to the unemployed, to ordinary members of congregations. Having listened, they go on to represent their views in theological debates. Listening is essential but it should lead to the third vital issue of giving people a voice so that they can express their own views, using their own language in their own thought forms in their own way.

There can be no doubt that hymns, with all that they carry about the Christian faith, are more familiar to many than the Bible. Even within the Christian faith, they occupy a large part of most acts of worship: if a service of one hour has five hymns, then approximately twenty minutes (a third of the service) will be spent singing them. The challenge that they bring concerns not only the liturgy of the Church but also the mission of God.

9

Whither Hymnody?

Reverence is due to hymns as to any sacred object. The hymn that revolts me, if it has been a means of grace to Christian men and women, I must respect as I should respect a communion cup, however scratched its surface, however vulgar its decoration.

B. L. Manning

Hymns are songs of the community and yet they are very personal. The hymn that one person may love, another may abhor. The hymn that one person associates with an occasion of joy, another may associate with an occasion of sadness. In this chapter we shall consider how hymns may be assessed, and shall go on to conjecture about the future of hymnody from the perspective of their potential as barometers of theology and spirituality.

It is difficult to make a critical assessment of a hymn without running the risk of belittling the faith of a person for whom that hymn has meant a great deal. But assessments and judgements need to be made and the overarching question must surely be: Is the hymn *true*? Before making any assessment, however, the hymn should be sung, preferably in the context for which it was intended.

Is the Hymn True to Itself

Dr Johnson in the *Life of Waller* divorced religion and poetry on the grounds that the deep relationship of the soul with God was on a plain above poetry and any attempt to give it poetic expression necessarily failed. Hymns, asserted Johnson, tended to be pious verses and they reached poetry purely by accident.

John Wesley thought in similar vein as the Preface to the *Collection of Hymns for the Use of People called Methodists* reveals:

> That which is of infinitely more moment than the Spirit of Poetry, is the Spirit of Piety. And I trust, all persons of real judgement will find this breathing through the whole Collection. It is in this view chiefly, that I would recommend it to every truly pious Reader, as a means of raising or quickening the spirit of devotion; of confirming his faith; of enlivening his hope; and of kindling and increasing his love to God and man. When Poetry thus keeps its place, as the handmaid of Piety, it shall attain, not a poor perishable wreath, but a crown that fadeth not away.[1]

Nineteenth-century hymn-writer James Montgomery (author of 'Hail to the Lord's Anointed' and 'Palms of Glory Raiment Bright') disagreed and tried to encourage a more 'literary' hymn which achieved higher poetic standards. Public school hymn books and *Songs of Praise*, which form a group of their own, make use of literary hymns, but they are rarely found in parish collections. Certainly the compilers of the 1861 *Hymns Ancient and Modern* rejected the pressure which wanted every hymn to be good poetry.

There have also been struggles over the music which accompanies hymns. To give hymns a more popular appeal, the Wesleys wanted them sung to folk tunes. Other hymns have been set to the plainsong of the medieval Church. Vaughan Williams tried to reclaim the English folk tradition in some of the tunes in the *English Hymnal*, the Twentieth Century Light Music Group composed music in the style of Gershwin and Cole Porter while others like Holst and Charles Wood drew on a more classical tradition. Musicians will comment on the qualities of a hymn tune as poets will on the quality of the lyrics, but does that bring us any closer to a way of assessing the hymn? Dr Colin Morris, in a sermon given in Westminster Abbey to celebrate the thirtieth anniversary of BBC's *Songs of Praise*, provides a clue for hymn assessment:

> Let the professors of music sniffily declare a tune banal or sentimental; let the theologians loftily pronounce the words

doggerel or even heretical; but if the people take that hymn to their hearts, sooner or later it will triumph.[2]

The implication of Morris' comments is that hymns are not poetry nor are they music but they are an inseparable mixture of the two creating a form which is unique. If any person questions this inseparability of words and music let that person try asking a congregation to sing a well-loved hymn to an unfamiliar tune! People were not happy in the 1960s when the Twentieth Century Light Music Group set hymns like 'Holy, Holy, Holy', 'At the Name of Jesus' and 'Now Thank We All Our God' to unfamiliar tunes, though 'Lord Jesus Christ' was received well because it was a new tune for new words. The editors of *Hymns for Today's Church* (1982) received criticism for daring to tinker in a minor way with the words of familiar hymns, changing, for example, 'O come, all ye faithful' to 'O come, all you faithful' and 'The strife is o'er, the battle done' to 'The strife is past, the battle done'. The mark of a good hymn is the marriage of words and tune and this marriage is indissoluble.

Nevertheless, in order to express their thoughts, hymn-writers follow the fashions of writing prevalent at the time and so it is important to assess their writing in the light of whether they have been effective in their expression. In a similar way, the music to which the hymn is being sung needs to be subject to scrutiny. If those singing the hymn feel that there is anything second rate about a hymn as regards the words or music, it is important that questions are asked. Such questions may well spring from the way in which God has been experienced through music and poetry and a genuine engaging of these questions with hymns is an engaging of faith with the world. The hymn-writer is engaged in theology and the question is: How can music and poetry of any style express the truth the hymn-writer is wanting to convey and how can the theologian's method of communication be helped, modified and challenged by the musician and poet. But in the end, the hymn-writer is not seeking a poem, nor a tune, but the hymn-writer is searching for a hymn.

Is the Hymn True to its Purpose?

In a broadcast on the BBC Home Service in 1952, Erik Routley, exploring the question of what makes a good hymn, said
that just as a sea-shanty was judged by asking whether it was
effective in its purpose of helping sailors heave the capstan and
a military march is judged by its effectiveness in helping the
soldiers march properly, so too a hymn needs to be judged by
its effectiveness in helping people worship.[3] Worshippers may
feel encouraged, inspired or challenged after singing – this is
the marks of a good hymn. They may feel discouraged, despon-
dent or depressed after singing – this is not the mark of a
good hymn, though it may be the mark of a good hymn badly
presented.

Is the Hymn True to God's Purpose?

A hymn also needs to be considered in the way it enables the
singer to be involved with God's world. The Church is called
to worship God which it does effectively when it engages with
the world. How does the hymn view humanity and the world?
Does it encourage the singer into the world or does it encourage
the singer to remain unchallenged within the Church community?

Is the Hymn True to Jesus Christ?

A hymn should be assessed by whether it is true to the Christ
it sets out to expound. Fanny Crosby, author of 'To God be
the Glory', wrote the hymn:

> Behold Me standing at the door,
> And hear me pleading evermore,
> With gentle voice: oh, heart of sin,
> May I come in? May I come in?
>
> I bring thee joy from heaven above,
> I bring thee pardon, peace and love;
> Say, weary heart, oppressed with sin,
> May I come in? May I come in?[4]

This hymn is not consistent with the Christ in the Gospels, who offers forgiveness even before it is sought and it certainly militates against the doctrine of grace. The hymn is endeavouring to foster the singer's dependence on Christ and in so doing is distorting the Gospel.

Is the Hymn True to its Context?

Hymns are written for specific occasions and are meant to be sung at particular points in the service. How effective are hymns in their settings?

Charles Wesley's

> Author of life divine,
> Who hast a table spread,
> Furnish'd with mystic Wine
> And everlasting Bread. . .

was written for *Hymns on the Lord's Supper* (1745) and was clearly meant to be sung at Holy Communion. Set within the Scripture readings and the prayers required to be said at Holy Communion, this hymn frees the worshipper for wider meditation on God's gifts. Outside Holy Communion, the hymn will mean very little. In a similar way the Iona hymn 'I am the Vine and You the Branches' was written as a paraphrase of John 15.1–17 and works best when sung as a reflection on this passage. These hymns would need to be assessed within the setting for which they were intended, so we should not be surprised if some hymns, like plants, cannot be uprooted and moved from where they were originally intended to be. For example, Richard Jones' 'God of Concrete, God of Steel' which was radical in the 1960s, loses its power in a society where the industries which are at the heart of the hymn are no longer a significant part of the national landscape. What is so encouraging is that many hymns are sufficiently versatile to be used on occasions other than those for which they were originally written. The hymns that seem to withstand 'transplanting' particularly well are those with clear Scriptural allusions such as 'Guide Me, O Thou Great Redeemer' with its references to the trials and journeys of the people of Israel under the leadership of

Moses or 'Praise, My Soul, the King of Heaven' based on Psalm 103 and conveying God's loving nature. All of the hymns of Isaac Watts and the majority of those of Charles Wesley which the editors of *Hymns Ancient and Modern New Standard* (1983) use, believing them to have contemporary relevance, have strong Scriptural allusions. Hymns based on Scripture, with which the singer may be familiar, provide a 'meeting place' for the singer and author other than the latter's cultural background and experience with which the singer may not be familiar: the common 'meeting place' provided by the Scriptural allusions joins singer and author as they both become involved with the text.

Is the Hymn True to its Singers?

One of the reasons for the versatility of hymns is the adaptability of the language. This is a feature of folk-songs. It is, however, very important that the language of hymns be adapted sensitively. The Preface to the *Collection of Hymns*, written by John Wesley, shows that he and his brother Charles had a difficult time with bad adaptations:

> And here I beg leave to mention a thought which has been long upon my mind, and which I should long ago have inserted in the public papers, had I not been unwilling to stir up a nest of hornets. Many gentlemen have done my Brother and me (though without naming us) the honour to reprint many of our Hymns. Now they are perfectly welcome so to do, provided they print them just as they are. But I desire they would not attempt to mend them: for really they are not able. None of them is able to mend either the sense, or the verse. Therefore I must beg of them one of these two favours: either to let them stand just as they are, to take them for better for worse: or to add the true reading in the margin, or at the bottom of the page; that we may no longer be accountable either for the nonsense or for the doggerel of other men.[5]

Significantly, John Wesley himself was not above altering the 'sense and verse' of others.

Language may be changed to make words more acceptable;

for example, in verse 4 of Augustus Toplady's 'Rock of Ages'
we sing:

> While I draw this fleeting breath,
> When my eyelids close in death.

But the original was:

> While I draw this fleeting breath,
> When my eye-strings break in death.

Language may also be changed to make a hymn accessible.
An increasing number of women have felt excluded through
the use of exclusive masculine language, words like 'mankind'
and 'men' being used to refer to men and women and 'he'
frequently being used to refer to God. Thoughtless use of
language can alienate and, in our case, make hymns less accessible. Modern hymn books that do not, as far as they are able,
ensure that the language is inclusive have failed to understand
how, in order to continue to express truth, hymns have been
adapted. An example of such adaptation can be seen in *Rejoice
and Sing*'s rendering of verses 2 and 5 of 'All My Hope on God
is Founded': where the words

> Pride of man and earthly glory,
> sword and crown betray his trust . . .

> Still from man to God eternal
> sacrifices of praise be done . . .

are changed to

> Human pride and earthly glory,
> sword and crown betray our trust . . .

> Still from earth to God eternal
> sacrifice of praise be done . . .

Of course, it is not possible for all hymns to be adapted in
this way. Even *Rejoice and Sing*, which goes to great lengths to
change the language while retaining the poetry, could not alter
verse 5 of 'Praise to the Holiest in the Height':

> O generous love! That he who smote
> in man for man the foe,
> the double agony in man
> for man should undergo.

In such cases as this we are left with the dilemma of either
omitting the verse, which would affect the coherence of the
whole hymn, completely rewriting the verse, or leaving it
unaltered. This would be a matter for debate within a worshipping community. The issue of referring to God in inclusive
language needs to be part of this debate.

Is the Hymn True to Human Nature?

Hymns provide channels through which the emotions are
expressed in worship. We need to beware, however, that the
emotional content is not given free rein so that the intellect and
even the will are by-passed. Faith suffers if it is dominated by
the emotional side of human nature, just as it suffers if dominated by the rational. If unchecked, the emotional power of
hymns can be a hindrance to the truth of the Gospel towards
which the hymns should be pointing. Instead of encouraging
us forwards to explore worship and truth, hymns, when abused,
can hold us back and turn us in on ourselves, bathing us in
nostalgia and 'nice' feelings. This is where the importance of
other, less emotional, forms of theology becomes apparent.
Another way of guarding against the excesses of emotion is to
ensure that new hymns from a variety of traditions are sung: a
congregation which is reluctant to face the challenge of new
hymns is reluctant to grow. Estelle White in her hymn 'Moses,
I Know You're the Man' writes in the second verse:

> 'Don't get too set in your ways,' the Lord said;
> 'each step is only a phase,' the Lord said.[6]

The Future of Hymnody

Can we draw any conclusions about the future of hymns? Men
and women will always want to sing their faith and so the future
of hymnody is assured, but what kind of future will it be?

We have already viewed hymns as 'barometers', providing a

synthesis of where a church has reached in its theology and
spirituality and in its relationship with culture. There are four
major stages through which hymns have passed. First, the early
hymns were 'objective' in the way that they reflected upon the
sacred story, though the language and symbols they employed
made sense in their own contexts, no doubt reflecting the concerns and priorities of the Church. 'The Royal Banners Forward Go' and 'Sing, My Tongue, the Glorious Battle' illustrate
this stage well.

Secondly, with the sacred story as the pivot of the hymn,
there were reflections on the human response to God's actions,
as Watts' 'When I Survey the Wondrous Cross' shows:

> His dying crimson like a robe,
> Spreads o'er his body on the Tree;
> Then am I dead to all the globe,
> And all the globe is dead to me.

Thirdly, the secondary theme, the human response to God's
actions, became more prominent, deposing the sacred story.
This was particularly true in the Victorian period, as in Samuel
Longfellow's (1819–92) hymn 'I Look to Thee in Every Need':

> Discouraged in the work of life,
> Disheartened by its load,
> Shamed by its failures or its fears,
> I sink beside the road;
> But let me only think of thee,
> And then new heart springs up in me.

Finally, the sacred story was reinstated as a way of reflecting
the contemporary human condition thereby turning the secondary theme into the primary theme. This is well illustrated
by hymns sung at the time of the First World War as we have
seen in the hymn 'O Valiant Hearts'. Cecil Spring-Rice's 'I Vow
to Thee, My Country' is another illustration of this as devotion to one's country which results in the 'final sacrifice' of
death which will be rewarded by admission to another country':

I vow to thee, my country – all earthly things above –
Entire and whole and perfect the service of my love:

The love that asks no questions, the love that stands the test,
That lays upon the altar the dearest and the best . . .

And there's another country, I've heard of long ago,
Most dear to them that love her, most great to them that know . . .

There are contemporary examples of all these stages, pointing towards a growing pluralism within the Church. A popular
example of an 'objective' hymn is Timothy Dudley-Smith's
'Tell Out, My Soul, the greatness of the Lord'. Like the ancient
'objective' hymns, 'Tell Out, My Soul' reflects upon the sacred
story in language charged with contemporary meaning. In a
world which, in the last thirty-five years, has been made aware
of the plight of many in the southern hemisphere, the third
verse is especially poignant:

> proud hearts and stubborn wills are put to flight,
> the hungry fed, the humble lifted high.

The second stage, using the sacred story as the pivot of the
hymn with reflections on the human response, can be found in
Emily Chisholm's 'Peter Feared the Cross for Himself and his
Master' where the passion story is used to lead the singers into
a personal contemplation on their part in Christ's betrayal and
death:

> Pilate asked the crowd to set free their good Master.
> 'Crucify', they shouted, 'we don't want him back!'
> O Lord have mercy,
> lighten our darkness.
> We crucified you,
> our light is black.

Estelle White's 'Autumn Days When the Grass is Jewelled'
illustrates the third stage which deposes the sacred story and
concentrates on the human response to God's creation. This is
found in the book which is widely used by schools, *Come and
Praise*:

> Autumn days when the grass is jewelled
> And the silk inside a chestnut shell,

> Jet planes meeting in the air to be refuelled,
> All these things I love so well.
>
> *Chorus*: So I mustn't forget.
> No, I mustn't forget,
> To say a great big thank you,
> I mustn't forget.

Fred Kaan's 'Sing We a Song of High Revolt' illustrates the last stage. Kaan reinstates the sacred story, in this case, Mary's song of praise, the Magnificat, and uses it to illustrate the plight of the dispossessed and the outcome is:

> He calls us to revolt and fight
> with him for what is just and right . . .

This variety of contemporary hymns reveals the variety of ways in which men and women relate to the Christian faith. Hymns reflect different points of the pilgrimage of faith: some hymns can be more steeped in Scripture and tradition than others. Hymns from the first and second stages would be sung more frequently by men and women who were familiar with the sacred story and the Christian faith. The third stage is an attempt to express contemporary experience in 'God language' and would require no knowledge at all of Scriptures, but merely a belief that there was some ultimate being. The fourth stage, attempting to explain the world in terms of faith, requires a strong commitment to the world as God's earthly Kingdom. This stage concentrates on relationship with God, using the sacred story to communicate directly the fruits of such reflection.

There is undoubtedly a future for the hymn because human beings will always want to sing their faith. In the past, schools have played a key role in the hymnody of the Church. The charity schools and asylums were significant in introducing hymns into churches in the eighteenth and nineteenth centuries. The public schools played a key role in encouraging hymnody into the lives of those who were to be the rulers within society. The hymns sung in schools in the early 1960s are those frequently sung in churches today. Although today

hymns are rarely sung in secondary schools, they are alive and
well in many, though not all, primary schools. The hymns that
are sung do not tend to be those used in churches: assemblies
are required to be non-denominational in state schools and one
gets the impression that the hymns being sung, when they
actually speak about God, struggle for a language in which to
articulate God because traditional Scriptural images do not
embrace a multi-faith perspective. There will probably be more
hymns in which the sacred story is deposed since the symbols
of Scripture are not well known by our young people. If the
hymns to be sung in Church in thirty years' time are those
currently being sung in school, then there will be a repertoire of
hymns upon which the sacred story does not impinge. Christian
communities have a duty and joy to cherish and foster hymnody
old and new – and to ensure that this tradition continues
through the encouragement of new hymns.

At the end of the day, it is not the symbolism or language
that carry them, but the conviction of those who sing and write
the hymns. Do we identify with the aspirations of the writers,
feeling challenged or exhilarated by them, or do we feel
untouched and unmoved? It is this that forms our attitude
towards particular hymns – and as communities and individuals, we are all different.

Notes

1 The Power of the Hymn

1 D. B. Barrett, 'Annual Statistical Table on Global Mission', *International Bulletin of Missionary Research* 14 (January 1990), 26.
2 See Ian Bradley, *The Times*, Monday 29 May 1989, p. 16.
3 See 'ITV's off-peak "Godslot" criticised', *The Independent*, 26 January 1994.
4 Op. cit. p. 1.
5 Quoted from John Julian, *A Dictionary of Hymnology*, p. 207.
6 'Church Hymns' (folio ed. 1881), quoted in Julian, *op. cit.*, p. 7.
7 *Op. cit.*, p. 136.
8 'African Affairs' 53 (1954), 234–41, quoted from A. P. Merriam, *The Anthropology of Music*, p. 237.
9 A. P. Merriam, *The Anthropology of Music*, pp. 13, 201 and 207.
10 E. Routley, *An English-Speaking Hymnal Guide*. p. i.
11 I. Bradley, *Op. cit.*, p. 10.
12 Quoted in L. E. Elliott-Binns, *Religion in the Victorian Era*, p. 374.

2 Hymns and Theology

1 For a fuller treatment see W. J. Hollenweger, 'Intercultural Theology', *Theological Renewal*, 10 (October 1978) pp. 2–13.
2 Some historians suggest the hymn may have been written as early as 1630.
3 D. MacCulloch, *Groundwork of Christian History*, p. 93.
4 D. Tutu, 'Whither African Theology?' in E. W. Fashole-Luke, A. Hastings and G. Tasie (eds), *Christianity in Independent Africa*, p. 369.
5 Hollenweger, *op. cit.*, p. 4.
6 A&MNS 370.
7 B. C. Castle, *Hymns: The Making and Shaping of a Theology for the Whole People of God*, p. 236, no. 17.

8   Robin Gill (ed.), *Theology and Sociology – A Reader*, p. 265.
9   See L. and C. Boff, *Introducing Liberation Theology*, pp. 34–5, for more detail.
10 *Sent by the Lord*, p. 37.
11 Castle, *op. cit.*, p. 238, no. 25.
12 For a fuller exposition see G. Rowell, *Hell and the Victorians*, p. 18f.

3   From Psalmody to Negro Spirituals

1   *Confessions*, IX, 7.
2   This hymn is known as 'Veni, redemptor gentium' and can be found in the A&M Historical edition 55. It is mentioned in St Augustine, *Sermon*, CCCLXXII, 4.3.
3   Corpus Christi College, Cambridge, MS 298, f. 20v, quoted in Greene, *The Early English Carols*, p. cxvi.
4   Greene, no. 52.
5   *Ibid.*, no. 11.
6   *Ibid.*, p. xciii.
7   Quoted in Julian, *op. cit.*, p. 859.
8   See T. Ingram and D. Newton, *Hymns as Poetry*, p. 14.
9   Watts, 'Hymns and Spiritual Songs', quoted Ingram and Newton, *op cit.*, p. 15.
10 Manning, *op. cit.*, pp. 98–9.
11 *Ibid.*, pp. 99–100.
12 See Chapter 1, p. 18 for more detail on this hymn.
13 *Op. cit.*, p. 225.
14 See John R. Tyson, *Charles Wesley – A Reader*, p. 21.
15 *Ibid.*, p. 13.
16 *Life and Letters of James Martineau*, Vol. II, p. 99, New York 1902, quoted in Benson, *op cit.*, p. 249.
17 C. Wesley, 'Hymns and Sacred Poems,' quoted in Tyson, *op cit.*, p. 221. The capitalization and spelling of the original has been preserved.
18 Preface to the book, p. iv, 1780 edition in the Bodleian Library, Oxford.
19 Jackson, 'Charles Wesley's Journal', II, pp. 31–2, quoted in Tyson, *op. cit.*, p. 17.
20 This hymn can be found in most Methodist hymn books.
21 *Op. cit.*, no. 470.
22 Cone, *op. cit.*, pp. 4–5.

4   From 'Amazing Grace!' to 'O Valiant Hearts'

1   Quoted in *Hymns Ancient and Modern* – Historical edition, p. xciv.
2   Both verses are quoted in L. Adey's, *Class and Idol in the English Hymn*, pp. 113 and 115.
3   Quoted in W. K. Lowther Clarke, *One Hundred Years of Hymns Ancient and Modern*, p. 1.
4   *Ibid.*, p. 24, from a letter of W. H. Baker dated 15 December 1858.
5   The numbers refer to *Hymns Ancient and Modern*, Standard edition, published in 1924, which is based on the 1875 edition with supplements.
6   Details of this book, housed in the John Rylands Library in Manchester, come from an article by Neil Dixon in *Hymn Society Bulletin* 120 (January 1971), 105–9.
7   Quoted in Adey, *Class and Idol in the English Hymn*, p. 158.
8   See details of research in Adey, *op. cit.*, pp. 170 and 263ff.
9   *Sacred Songs and Solos*, nos. 945, 957, 1017.

5   The Hymn Explosion

1   The author is indebted to an article by Eric Sharpe in *Hymn Society Bulletin* for the title of this chapter, though the period has been changed – see, '1970–1980: The Explosive Years for Hymnody in Britain', *Hymn Society Bulletin* 153 (January 1982), 9–20.
2   J. A. T. Robinson, *Honest to God*, pp. 7–8.
3   These statistics are provided by the Central Board of Finance of the Church of England and can be found in the *Church of England Year Book*, 1991, pp. 400–1.
4   This information was taken from Bernard Braley, *Hymnwriters*, vol. 3, p. 135. These books provide a great wealth of information about hymn-writers from Thomas Ken to today.
5   *Thirty 20th Century Hymn Tunes*, p. 2.
6   *Op. cit.*, p. 435.
7   *Op. cit.*, p. 216.
8   *Op. cit.*, p. 39.
9   Sources of Carter's hymns: *Hymns Ancient and Modern, New Standard*, pp. 375 and 433, and *Faith, Hope and Festivity*, p.12.
10 Source of Kaan's hymns: *Rejoice and Sing* 195, 620 and 89.
11 *Hymns and Songs*, 74.
12 *Heaven Shall Not Wait*, pp. 124 and 89.
13 *Hymns and Psalms*, 343.

14 These hymns can be found in *Combined Sound of Living Waters – Fresh Sounds*, pp. 414, 280, 390, 372, 368 and 369.

15 Taizé issues its 'Chants de Taizé' annually. These are taken from a selection. Translations were supplied by Taizé.

16 *Iona Community Wild Goose Songs*, Vol. I, pp. 25 and 117; Vol. II pp. 91 and 121.

17 See G. Kendrick, *The Collection*, 9, 17 and 48.

18 Ibid., 56, 57, 12, 41 and 48.

19 No. 18.

20 J. Davies, *The Faith Abroad*, p. 127.

6 Hymns Within Worship

1 *Hymns Ancient and Modern*, 384, v. 4.

2 *Rejoice and Sing*, 555.

3 *Hymns Ancient and Modern*, New Standard, 106.

4 *Rejoice and Sing*, 625.

5 A&MNS, 131.

6 *Hymns of Wesley and Watts*, p. 133.

7 A&MNS, p. v.

8 *New English Hymnal*, p. v.

9 *The Music of the English Church*, p. 401.

10 *Songs of Praise*, nos. 396 and 640.

11 *New English Hymnal*, 307.

12 A&MNS, 289 vv. 1 and 3.

13 *Singing the Faith*, pp. 131–2.

14 *A Collection of Hymns for People called Methodists*, p. iv.

15 *Methodist Hymn Book*, 23.

16 MHB, 2.

17 *Rejoice and Sing*, 95.

18 *Rejoice and Sing*, 146 omits this verse.

19 *Congregational Praise*, 329

20 *Rejoice and Sing*, 641.

21 This document (known as BEM) was finally agreed in Lima, Peru, in 1982, and represents a significant theological convergence which had been discerned among member churches. BEM is the fruit of a process which can be dated back to the WCC 'Faith and Order' Conference at Lausanne in 1927.

22 *Westminster Hymnal* received an 'imprimatur' (the official sanction of the Church) whereas other subsequent Catholic hymnals have not.

23 See the document 'Musicam Sacram', 1967.

24   *New Catholic Hymnal,* p. ix.
25   *Celebration Hymnal,* Vol. 2. nos. 546 and 549.
26   See B. Castle, *Hymns: The Making and Shaping of a Theology for the Whole People of God,* p. 238. The translation was made by a Zambian who sings these hymns and, in order to retain some of the flavour of the language, has not been altered.
27   For a fuller discussion see my article, 'Hymns – More than Songs of Praise', *Theology* XCIV (March/April 1991), 101–6.
28   See J. T. Slater, *Bulletin of the University of Leeds Institute of Education,* November 1961, reprinted in *Hymn Society Bulletin* (100) Spring 1994, p. 205.
29   See article by G. Wrayford in *Hymn Society Bulletin* (140), October 1977, p. 237.
30   *Come and Praise,* nos. 50 and 53.

7 Hymns Without Worship

1   Quoted in I. Bradley (ed.), *The Penguin Book of Hymns,* p. 309. Details of the story have been drawn from the same source.
2   M. Marshall, *Church at the Crossroads – Lambeth 1988,* p. xi.

8 Sing a New Song to the Lord

1   W. J. Hollenweger, 'Music in the Service of Reconciliation', *Theology,* XCII (July 1989), 279.
2   Thodberg, 'Grundtvig the Hymnwriter' in *N. F. S. Grundtvig, Tradition and Renewal,* quoted in J. R. Watson, 'Grundtvig and the English Hymn' in Allchin et al. (eds), *Heritage and Prophecy,* p. 117.
3   *The Alternative Service Book 1980,* p. 362.
4   J. B. Webster, 'Ministry and Priesthood' in S. Sykes and J. Booty (eds.), *The Study of Anglicanism,* p. 293.
5   D. Tutu, *Crying in the Wilderness,* p. 35.
6   A quotation from Dr Emmanuel Lartey to be found in an article by Walter Hollenweger in *International Review of Mission,* LXXVI (October 1987), 531.
7   Carl Rogers, 'On Becoming a Better Person' (Boston: Houghton Miffin Co., 1962), p. 333, quoted in Bakan, 'Duality', p. 99, quoted in Wink, *The Bible in Human Transformation,* pp. 33–4.

9 Whither Hymnody?

1 *Op. cit.*, p. vi.
2 The address was given on 30 September 1991.
3 The talk is reproduced in *Hymn Society Bulletin* 63 (Spring 1973), 90ff.
4 *Sacred Songs and Solos*, 378.
5 *Op. cit.*, p. vi.
6 *Baptist Praise and Worship*, 489.

Select Bibliography

Adey, Lionel, *Class and Idol in the English Hymn*, Vancouver, University of British Columbia, 1988.

Ade, Lionel, *Hymns and the Christian Myth*, Vancouver, University of British Colombia, 1986.

Allchin, Jasper et al. (eds), *Heritage and Prophecy – Grundtvig and the English-Speaking World*, Norwich, The Canterbury Press, 1994.

The Alternative Service Book 1980 Clowes/Cambridge University Press, SPCK, 1980.

Benson, Louis, *The English Hymn*, London, Hodder and Stoughton, 1915.

Boff, L. & C., *Introducing Liberation Theology*, Kent, Burns & Oates, 1987.

Bradley, Ian (ed.), *The Penguin Book of Hymns*, London, Viking, 1989.

Braley, Bernard, *Hymnwriters 1–3*, London, Stainer and Bell, 1987, 1989 and 1991.

Carter, Sydney, *The Rock of Doubt*, London, Mowbray, 1978.

Castle, Brian, *Hymns: the making and shaping of a theology for the whole people of God*, Studies in the Intercultural History of Christianity, 67, Frankfurt am Main, Peter Lang Verlag, 1990.

Church of England Year Book, London, Central Board of Finance of the Church of England, 1991.

Clarke, W. K. Lowther, *A Hundred Years of Hymns Ancient and Modern*, London, Wm. Clowes, 1960.

Cone, J. H., *The Spirituals and the Blues*, New York, Seabury Press, 1972.

Davies, John D., *The Church Abroad*, Oxford, Basil Blackwell, 1983.

Edrington, R., *Everyday Men: Living in a climate of unbelief*, Studies in the Intercultural History of Christianity, Frankfurt am Main, Peter Lang Verlag, 1987.

Elliott-Binns, L. E., *Religion in the Victorian Era*, London, Lutterworth Press, 1946.

Fashole-Luke, E. W., Hastings, A., and Tasie, G., (eds), *Christianity in Independent Africa*, London, Rex Collings, 1978.

Gilbert, A. D., *Religion and Society in Industrial England: Church, Chapel and Social Change 1740–1914*, London, Longman, 1984.

Gill, R. (ed.), *Theology and Sociology – A Reader*, London, Geoffrey Chapman, 1987.

Greene, R. L. (ed.), *The Early English Carols*, Oxford, Clarendon Press, 1935.

Hardy, Daniel and Ford, David, *Jubilate – Theology in Praise*, London, Darton, Longman & Todd, 1984.

The Bulletin of the Hymn Society of Great Britain and Ireland – Various Editions.

Julian, John (ed.), *A Dictionary of Hymnology*, 2nd edn, 1907, rep London: John Murray, 1915.

Long, Kenneth R., *The Music of the English Church*, London, Hodder and Stughton, 1972.

MacCulloch, D., *Groundwork of Christian History*, London, Epworth Press, 1987.

Mackenzie, I., *Tunes of Glory*, Carberry, Handsel Press, 1993.

Manning, B., *The Hymns of Wesley and Watts*, London, Epworth Press, 1942. Reissued 1988.

Marshall, M., *Church at the Crossroads – Lambeth 1988*, London, Collins, 1988.

Merriam, Alan P., *The Anthropology of Music*, Evanston, USA, Northwestern University Press, 1964.

Robertson, C. (ed.), *Singing the Faith – Essays by members of the Joint Liturgical Group on the use of hymns in liturgy*, Norwich, The Canterbury Press, 1990.

Routley, Erik, *An English-Speaking Hymnal Guide*, Collegeville, USA, Minnesota Liturgical Press, 1979.

Routley, Eric, *The Church and its Music*, London, Gerald Duckworth & Co. Ltd., 1967.

Robinson, J., *Honest to God*, London, SCM, 1963.

Rowell, G., *Hell and the Victorians*, Oxford, Clarendon Press, 1974.

Sykes, S. & Booty, J. (eds), *The Study of Anglicanism*, London, SPCK, 1988.

Tutu, D., *Crying in the Wilderness*, London, Mowbray, 1982.

Thurman, H., *Deep River and The Negro Spiritual Speaks of Life and Death*, Richmond, Indiana, Friends United Press, 1975.

Tyson, John R., *Charles Wesley – A Reader*, Oxford, Oxford University Press, 1989.

Wink, W., *The Bible in Human Transformation*, Philadelphia, Fortress Press, 1973.

Wilson, S., 'Religious attitudes in Hymns Ancient and Modern (1889), *Social Compass*, XXII (1975/2), 212–36.

Wilson-Dickson, A., *The Story of Christian Music*, Oxford, Lion Publishing, 1992.

Hymn Books

Anglican Hymn Book, London, Clowes, 1965.

Baptist Praise and Worship, Oxford, Oxford University Press, 1992.

Celebration Hymnal Vols. 1 and 2, Great Wakering, Mayhew-McCrimmon, 1978 and 1984.

Chants de Taizé, France, Taizé, 1991.

Combined Sound of Living Waters – Fresh Sounds, London, Hodder and Stoughton, 1978.

Come and Praise, London, BBC Books, 1986.

Faith, Folk and Festivity, London, Galliard (Stainer & Bell), 1969.

Hymns Ancient and Modern, Historical Edition, London, Wm. Clowes, 1909.

Hymns Ancient and Modern, Standard Edition, London, Wm. Clowes & Sons Ltd., 1924.

Hymns Ancient and Modern, New Standard, Hymns Ancient & Modern Ltd., 1984.

Hymns for Today's Church, London, Hodder and Stoughton, 1987.

Hymns and Psalms, London, Methodist Publishing House, 1983.

Hymns and Songs, London, Methodist Publishing House, 1969.

Hymns for Today's Church, London, Hodder and Stoughton, 1982.

Hymns of the City, Sheffield, Urban Theology Unit, 1989.

Kendrick, G., *The Collection*, Eastbourne, Kingsway Music, 1992.

Sent by the Lord, Glasgow, Wild Goose Publications/Iona Community, 1991.

Mission Praise – Mission England Praise, Marshall, Morgan and Scott, 1983.

New Catholic Hymnal, London, Faber Music, 1971.

New Songs of Celebration, Great Wakering, McCrimmon Publishing Co. Ltd., 1989.

Sacred Songs and Solos: Revised and Enlarged with Standard Hymns, Compiled by Ira D. Sankey, London, Marshall, Morgan and Scott.

The Westminster Hymnal, London, Burns & Oates Ltd., 1964.

Thirty Twentieth Century Hymn Tunes, London, Josef Weinberger, 1964.

Wild Goose Songs, Vols. 1, 2 & 3, Glasgow, Wild Goose Publications/Iona Community, 1989, 1990 and 1989.

Index of Hymns

This index contains those hymns whose title line is quoted in the text.